THE HIDDEN LIFE OF PRAYER

IN TODAY'S ENGLISH AND WITH A STUDY GUIDE

DAVID M. MCINTYRE

GODLIPRESS TEAM

© **Copyright 2022 by GodliPress. All rights reserved.**

This book is copyright protected. It is only for personal use. You cannot amend, distribute, sell, use, quote or paraphrase any part, or the content within this book, without the consent of the author or publisher, except in the case of brief quotations embodied in critical articles or reviews.

Scripture quotations are from The ESV® Bible (The Holy Bible, English Standard Version®), copyright © 2001 by Crossway, a publishing ministry of Good News Publishers. Used by permission. All rights reserved

CONTENTS

Introduction	v
1. THE LIFE OF PRAYER	1
Study Guide	11
2. THE EQUIPMENT	13
A Quiet Place	14
A Quiet Hour	17
A Quiet Heart	20
Study Guide	24
3. THE DIRECTION OF THE MIND	26
Realize the Presence of God	27
Honesty in Prayer	30
Faith	34
Study Guide	38
4. THE ENGAGEMENT—WORSHIP	40
Acknowledgment of Daily Mercy	42
Thanksgiving for Redemption	45
Contemplation of Godly Perfection	49
Study Guide	51
5. THE ENGAGEMENT—CONFESSION	53
Study Guide	61
6. THE ENGAGEMENT—REQUEST	64
Study Guide	72
7. THE HIDDEN RICHES OF THE SECRET PLACE	75
Study Guide	83
8. THE OPEN REWARD	85
Study Guide	96

Footnotes	99
About David McIntyre	111
References	115

INTRODUCTION

Much has been written on prayer, from almost every angle possible. Visiting a Christian bookshop and searching under this topic will give you an overdose of titles from which to choose. Even David McIntyre agrees that perhaps we are spoilt for choice. So, why is this one necessary? In his own words, he says, "it seems to me that there is still room for one in which an appeal may be taken, steadily, and from every point to life—to the experience of God's saints."

He wrote a number of other books, but he is best known for the volume you are holding in your hands right now: *The Hidden Life of Prayer*. This one shines as a beacon across the ages. It stacks up alongside the other great classics that pastors, teachers, and serious Christians go to for inspiration, guidance, and help. It's the reason for publishing an updated version of this timeless work.

If there was one sentence to encapsulate McIntyre's strong motivation for us to learn how and when to pray, it would be from his own words: "No duty is more earnestly impressed on us in Scripture than the duty of continual communion with Him."

He doesn't make any attempt to explain the mechanics and the mysteries of how prayer works, other than to accept that it is a vital part of the Christian life—vital enough that without it, you will not mature or grow closer to God. What he does do, in his academic style, is draw from the incredible background of others who have tried, failed, and learned its secrets. His angle is that it is best to learn from those experienced enough to have walked the same path and succeeded.

Possibly, another reason why this small book stands above the rest that have been written on the same subject is that his approach is not entirely intellectual or just biblically-based. He doesn't just quote verses and use as many examples of other prominent Christians as possible. Rather, he writes from experience. His own life has often been commended as one that was spent on its knees before the throne. Between the many great men of God that fill these pages, we find Mcintyre's personal commitment and passion for prayer shining through. We can sense his passion and his desire to stay in the upper room.

As a result, McIntyre's small book on the secret place of prayer and the treasures we find there has become a timeless classic. In this new edition, we have done our best to bring the same heart and passion into our modern era by adjusting outdated phrases and words. The meanings are the same.

The reason, that after a century, it is still a sought-after guide, is still in your hands—filled with rich anecdotes, tips, and biblical instruction.

To assist in this area, you will find a study guide with some questions. These are not meant to add incredible insight or take anything away from the book's reputation. Instead, it is purely to allow for a pause after each chapter, to reflect on what has been read, and in doing so, apply it to your own life.

David McIntyre's desire to enter into the secret place of prayer and find the treasures that are hidden there needs to become ours too. For when we find out the value of speaking with and listening to God, in the right way, we will see and reap the benefits. As in any relationship, it can only grow if there is communication.

Lord, teach us to pray.

1

THE LIFE OF PRAYER

"My God. Thy creature answers, Thee."
–Alfred de Musset.

"The love of Christ is my prayer book."
–Gerhard Tersteegen.

"Prayer is the key of heaven; the Spirit helps faith to turn this key."
–Thomas Watson.

In a cathedral in Northern Europe, there is an exquisite set of three panels that boldly represent the prayer life. The first of them reminds us of the apostolic instruction, *"Pray without ceasing"* (1 Thess 5:17). We see the front of a spacious temple that opens onto a market square that is filled with crowds of men, gesturing and making deals—all to get rich. But there is One, with a crown of thorns and a garment woven without seam, that moves silently through the noisy masses, turning the greediest heart to a holy fear.

The second panel displays the sections of the temple where we see the common worship of the church as ministers in white robes move about. They carry oil for the lamp, water for the ceremonial washing basin, and blood from the altar. With pure intentions, their eyes are turned towards the unseen glory of God, they fulfill the sacred duties they are called to do.

The third panel introduces us to the inner sanctuary. A solitary worshiper has entered through the veil, quiet and humble, he bows before the Shekinah presence of God. This represents the hidden life of prayer that Jesus spoke of when He said, *"But when you pray, go into your room and shut the door and pray to your Father who is in secret. And your Father who sees in secret will reward you"* (Matt. 6:6).

Jesus takes it for granted that His people will pray, and the Bible hints at the duty to pray rather than demanding it. We cry out for the living God because of a divine instinct that has been put inside us. Although this instinct can be squashed by sin, it becomes powerful through salvation.

THEOLOGIANS AND CHRISTIANS agree that this is part of the new life in Christ:

- Chrysostom said, "The just man does not stop from praying until he ceases to be just."

- Augustine stated, "He that loves little prays little, and he that loves much prays much."
- Richard Hooker said, "Prayer is the first thing by which a righteous life begins, and the last by which it ends."
- Pre la Combe also mentioned, "He who has a pure heart will never cease to pray, and he who will be constant in prayer shall know what it is to have a pure heart."
- Bunyan commented, "If you are not a praying person, you are not a Christian."
- Richard Baxter said, "Prayer is the breath of the new creature."
- George Herbert wrote, "Prayer...the soul's blood."

But even though our dependence on God is instinctive, the Bible emphasizes the duty of continual communion with Him more than anything else. The main reason for this continuous reminder is the difficulty of prayer. It is something that requires much effort, and in our attempt to maintain the spirit of prayer, we are called to wrestle against principalities and powers of darkness.

"Dear Christian reader," says Jacob Boehme, "to pray correctly is right, sincere work." Prayer is the most inspirational energy of which the human spirit is capable.[1] One aspect of it is glory and purity; and the other is work, effort, battle, and agony. Hands that are lifted up in prayer, grow tired before the fight is won. Strained muscles and heavy panting show our exhaustion. The burden that is placed on the heart is evident in the pained wrinkles on the forehead, even when the midnight air is cool.

Prayer is when our earthly hearts are lifted up into heaven. Our cleansed spirits can enter into the holiest place, behind the torn curtain, where we find the glory of God. It is where we see things invisible to human eyes, know the mind of the Spirit, and speak words that are beyond our understanding. "A man that truly prays one prayer," says Bunyan, "shall never again be able to express with his mouth or pen the unutterable desires, sense, affection, and longing that went to God in that prayer."

The apostles of the early church had incredible energy in intercession: "Battering the gates of heaven with storms of prayer," they took the kingdom of heaven by violence. The first Christians proved in the wilderness, dungeon, arena, and at the stake, the truth of Jesus' words, *"What he says will come to pass, it will be done for him"* (Mark 11:23). Their hearts went up to God in prayer as the fire of the altar rises to heaven.

Scholars of the Talmud agree that in the divine life, there are four things that require determination and effort; prayer is one of these. Someone who met the German writer, Gerhard Tersteegen, remarked, "It seemed to me as if he had gone straight into heaven, and had lost himself in God; but often when he had finished praying, he was as white as the wall."

David Brainerd notes that on one occasion when he found his heart "exceedingly enlarged" in prayer, he was "in such anguish, and pleaded with so much sincerity and persistence," that when he got up from his knees, he felt "extremely weak and overcome." "I could hardly walk straight," he said, "my joints were loose, sweat ran down my face and body, and my whole being seemed as if it would dissolve." Someone wrote about John Foster, who used to spend long nights in his chapel in prayer and worship, pacing back and forth because his spirit was agitated until his feet had worn a little track in the aisle.[2]

There are so many examples, but we can just look at the Bible to find a principle or instance of the type of effort that effective prayer requires. Just look at the Psalmist: *"Give me life according to your word... in your righteousness give me life...in your steadfast love give me life...according to your justice give me life... for your name's sake, O Lord, preserve my life,"* (Psalm 119:25, 40, 88, 149; 143:11). And Isaiah's complaint that *"there is no one who calls upon your name, who rouses himself to take hold of you."* Does this sound familiar? Do we know what it is to 'labor,' to 'wrestle,' and to 'agonize' in prayer?[3]

Another explanation for the difficulty and effort involved in prayer lies in the fact that we are spiritually hindered: There is "the noise of archers in the places of drawing water." (The interference of battle when we are looking to draw from the well). Paul reminds us that we will have to maintain our prayer energy *"against the authorities, against the cosmic powers over this present darkness, against the spiritual forces of evil in the heavenly places"* (Eph 6:12).

Dr. Andrew Bonar used to say that the same way the King of Syria commanded his captains to fight no one else but the King of Israel, so the prince of the power of the air, the Devil, seems to focus all his attack against the spirit of prayer. If he is victorious there, he has won the battle. Sometimes we are conscious of something demonic aimed at the prayer in our hearts; sometimes we are led into dry, desert experiences, and it's as if God is hiding His face; sometimes, when we work hard to bring every thought and imagination under obedience to Christ, we just find confusion and worry; sometimes our natural laziness is enough for the evil one to use to turn us away from prayer. It's because of all these things that we must be diligent and determined, alert like a guard who knows that people's lives are dependent on his courage and vigilance.[4]

"*And what I say to you I say to all: Stay awake!*" Jesus said to the disciples (Mark 13:37).

As soldiers of Christ, there are times we neglect our duties, not guarding the gift of prayer carefully. If you are reading this, and you know that your prayers are weak, there's no joy in communion, no repentance in confession, "*Remember therefore from where you have fallen; repent, and do the works you did at first*" (Rev 2:5).[5]

"*Oh, stars of heaven that fade and flame, Oh, whispering waves below!*

Was earth, or heaven, or I the same, a year, a year ago!

The stars have kept their home on high, The waves their regular flow;

The love is lost that once was I, a year, a year ago."[6]

THE ONLY REMEDY for this laziness is that we should rekindle our love, as the Church in Ephesus was reminded in

Revelations 2:1-7. Let's ask for a fresh gift of the Holy Spirit to wake up our lazy hearts, a new understanding of God's love. The Spirit will help our weaknesses, and the compassion of the Son of God will cover us with passion and desire like clothing, stirring us with an intense flame and filling our hearts with heaven.

We "*ought always to pray and not lose heart*" (Luke 18:1)—even though the danger of our pathetic spirit is always a problem. The soil in which the prayer of faith takes root is a life of continuous relationship with God, a life in which the windows of the heart are always open to heaven. We don't know how powerful prayer really is until our hearts are so consistently focused on God that we always think of Him when we are not consumed by earthly worries. Origen, the early Christian scholar from Alexandria, was said (in his words) to have a life that was "one unceasing supplication." This is the one way, above all others, that the Christian life is achieved. Communication between the believer and his Lord should never be interrupted.[7]

"The vision of God," says Bishop Westcott, "makes life a continuous prayer." In that vision, all temporary worries and concerns will work themselves out, and we will see their priorities according to spiritual matters. Generally, prayer is the sum of our service to God,[8] so that fulfilling our duty is our holy service, and the familiar saying, "Work is worship," is validated. "*I give myself to prayer*" (Psalm 109:4). "*In everything by prayer and supplication with thanksgiving*" (Phil 4:6).

In the Old Testament, a life of prayer is often described as a walk with God. Enoch walked in confidence, Abraham in righteousness, Elijah in faithfulness, the sons of Levi in peace and justice. The life of prayer is also spoken of as living with God, even as Joshua did not leave the Tabernacle or as certain craftsmen lived with a king as they worked. It is also defined as the heart entering the presence of God; as the planets rise into the light of the sun or a beautiful, fragrant flower reaches up towards the light. Prayer is sometimes described as all the senses tuned and devoted in reverence, love, and praise. As one clear note can bring a choir jarring voices into harmony, so the spiritual instinct brings the heart to fear the name of the Lord.

The most familiar, and perhaps the most impressive, description of prayer in the Old Testament, is in the many passages where communication and relationship with God are mentioned as waiting on Him. A great scholar has given a beautiful definition of waiting on God: "To wait is not merely to remain impassive. It is to expect—to look for with patience, and also with submission. It is to long for, but not impatiently; to look for, but not to fret at the delay; to watch for, but not restlessly; to feel that if He does not come we will acquiesce, and yet to refuse to let the mind acquiesce in the feeling that He will not come."[9] No one can say that such a life is unrealistic and pointless. The real world is not a logical covering; reality is spiritual things, and the earthly ones are just 'patterns' and correspondences. Who is as practical as God? Which human concentrated all His efforts on the situations and events He was going to face like Jesus? Those who pray well, work well. Those who pray most, achieve the greatest results.[10] To use the striking phrase of Johannes Tauler, "In God, nothing is hindered."

Developing the habit of prayer will secure its expression on all suitable occasions.

Almost everyone will pray in times of need. Moses stood on the shores of the Red Sea, surveying the panic that the Israelites faced as they realized that the chariots of Pharaoh were thundering down upon them. *"Why do you cry to Me?"* said the Lord (Ex 14:15). Nehemiah stood before King Artaxerxes, who saw his inward grief and said, *"Why is your face sad, seeing you are not sick? This is nothing but sadness of the heart"* (Neh 2:2). That question opened the door for Nehemiah to admit that he had spent three months praying. The burning desire that had risen to God in those slow months was summed up in one enthusiastic answer, *"So I prayed to the God of heaven"* (Neh 2:4).

A person whose life is spent in fellowship with God will constantly seek and find regular opportunities to approach the throne of grace. Believers bring everything before the cross—at the name of Jesus, their hearts soar in adoration and praise to heaven. The early Christians never met without saying a blessing; they never left without prayer. The saints of the Middle Ages used every incident to bring them to intercession—the shadow on the sundial, the church bell, the flight of a bird, the rising sun, or a falling leaf.

Sir Thomas Browne made a promise to himself that became well-known to those around him: "To pray in all places where I can find silence; in any house, highway, or street; that every street in this city may witness that I have not forgotten God and my Savior in it; and that every parish or town where I have been may say the same. To take the opportunity of praying on the sight of any church which I see, or pass by, as I ride about. To pray daily, and particularly for my sick patients, and for all sick people. And at the entrance into the house of the sick to say, "The peace and the mercy of God be on this house." After a sermon to make a prayer and desire a blessing, and to pray for the minister."

The person that lives in the spirit of prayer will spend much time in solitary and intimate communion with God. This deliberate act of prayer will be the source for fresh springs of devotion that flow through the day. Even though spending time with God is the energy of the renewed nature, our hearts "*cling to the dust*" (Psalm 119:25) and devotion can become formal—it's empty of anything spiritual and tires itself of doing external works. Jesus reminds us of this dangerous threat and advises us that the only defense against becoming insincere in our approach to God is through diligent, private prayer.[11]

During a meeting of sincere people gathered to worship, a servant of the Lord that they did not know very well, except by reputation, came in. "And after some time, he had waited on the Lord in spirit; he had an opportunity to speak, all being silent. He said by way of exhortation, 'Keep the Lord's watch.' These words, being spoken in the power of God, had their effect on all or most of the meeting so that they felt some great dread and fear on their spirits. After a little time, he spoke again, saying, 'What I say to you, I say to all, Watch.' Then he was silent again a little time, but the whole meeting, being sensible that this man was in some extraordinary spirit and power, were all wondering what kind of teaching this was, being such a voice that most of them had never heard before, that carried such great authority with it that they all needed to submit to its power."[12]

Soldier of Christ, you are in the enemy's country; "Keep the Lord's watch."

Study Guide

Whether you are reading this book on your own or in a group, you can use these questions as a guide for deeper discussion or self-reflection. They are not meant to be worked through as a rigid examination, but more as signposts pointing you to walk further on in the journey of discovering prayer. If you miss a question or get caught up on only one and miss the rest, that is fine! As long as you are honest and allow the Holy Spirit to open your eyes and heart to more of Jesus.

In this first chapter, the reason for prayer is outlined for us. Not only that but the misconceptions are discussed, as well as the honest admission of how difficult we sometimes find it to commit to this seemingly simple duty.

1. Have a look at the three panels of the cathedral that MacIntyre uses to describe the different prayer scenarios: outer temple, inner temple, and holiest place. Right now, in your prayer life, where would you be placed? Why?
2. As an exercise, list all these Christian duties in order of importance: going to church, giving money offerings, worship, and praise, prayer, reading the

Bible, reaching the lost. Explain why you have put certain points higher or lower than others.
3. The author states that prayer "requires much effort." Why do you think this is the case?
4. Do you think 'unceasing' and 'continuous' prayer is possible?
5. McIntyre describes prayer as a battle. Do you think this is an appropriate picture?
6. Read Ephesians 6: 10-20, the well-known passage on the armor of God. It is interesting that after listing all the parts of a soldier's outfit and weaponry, prayer is mentioned. Why do you think Paul included verse 18 in here?
7. There is much said about 'secret' and 'private' prayer in this chapter. What do you understand by the use of these terms?

2
THE EQUIPMENT

"Remember that in the Levitical Law there is a frequent commemoration and charge given of the two daily sacrifices, the one to be offered up in the morning and the other in the evening. These offerings by incense our holy, harmless, and undefiled High Priest has taken away, and instead every devout Christian is at the appointed times to offer up a spiritual sacrifice of prayer: for 'God is a Spirit, and they that worship Him must worship Him in spirit and in truth.' At these prescribed times, if you want your prayers to ascend up before God, you must withdraw from all outward occupations, to prepare for the inward and divine."
–Henry Vaughan, Silurist.

"God comes to me in silent hours, As As morning dew to summer flowers."
–Mechthild von Magdeburg.

"It will never be altogether well with us until we convert the universe

into a prayer room and continue in the Spirit as we go from place to place...The prayer-hour is left standing before God until the other hours come and stand beside it; then, if they are found to be a harmonious harmonious sisterhood, the prayer is granted."
–George Bowen.

"But when you pray, go into your room and shut the door and pray" (Matt 6:6).

"Of this type of prayer," says Walter Hilton of Thurgarton, "our Lord talks about in a picture: *'The fire on the altar shall be kept burning on it; it shall not go out. The priest shall burn wood on it every morning'* (Lev 6:12). The fire of love shall always be burning in the soul of a devout and clean man or woman, which is God's altar. And the priest shall every morning lay sticks and nourish the fire. This man shall nourish the fire of love in his heart by holy psalms, clean thoughts, and fervent desire, that it may not go out at any time."[13]

The equipment for the inner life of prayer is simple, although it might not always be so easily maintained. It consists particularly of a quiet place, a quiet hour, and a quiet heart.

A Quiet Place

For many of us, the first of these three requirements, a quiet place, is well within our reach. But there are tens of thousands of Christians who find it almost impossible to withdraw to the necessary privacy of a secret place. A stay-at-home mother in a crowded apartment, a student in city lodgings, a farmer in his living quarters, a soldier in barracks, a pupil at boarding school, these and many more may not always be able to find quiet and solitude. But "*your Father knows*" (Matt 6:8).

And it is encouraging to remember that the very Prince of pilgrims, Jesus, shared the same experience as all of these. In the carpenter's house in Nazareth, it seems as though there were at least nine people who lived there. This consists of Jesus, Mary, His mother, Joseph, His father, Jesus' four brothers, and at least two sisters. The place probably consisted mainly of a living room, the workshop, and an internal room that served as a store for all the daily provisions of kitchen utensils, firewood, etc. That gloomy corner had a latch on the inside, put in there by the carpenter's Son. That dark room was His private place of prayer, just as sacred as the cloud-wrapped shrine of the Presence in the Temple.[14]

Afterward, when Jesus had started His public ministry, there were times when it was difficult for Him to have any time on His own. He was often in the company of people who did not care for His needs or comfort and gave Him no room or place to go to be alone. When His spirit hungered for communion with His Father, He had to walk out into the wilderness and mountains:

"*Cold mountains and the midnight air*

Witnessed the fervor of His prayer."

AND WHEN HE had no home of His own, and He went to Jerusalem for the Feasts, His habit was to go to the olive garden of Gethsemane. Under the branches of some gnarled tree, which was already old in Isaiah's time, Jesus must have watched the stars through the soft summer night.

ANY PLACE MAY BECOME a private place of prayer and worship, as long as it is private and quiet. Isaac went into the fields to meditate. Jacob stayed on the eastern bank of the River Jabbok after everyone else had gone across; there, he wrestled with the Angel and overcame. Moses, hidden in a gap in the rocks of Horeb, saw the vanishing glory of Jehovah passing him by. Elijah sent Ahab down to eat and drink, while he himself withdrew to the lonely mountain of Carmel. Daniel spent a few weeks in intercession on the banks of the River Hiddekel, that once watered Paradise. And Paul, in order that he might have an opportunity for undisturbed meditation and prayer, walked all the way from Troas to Assos.

AND IF THERE is no place to physically go to, then the heart that turns to God can find quiet, even in the crowded areas or in the busy streets. A poor woman in a city, who wasn't able to get away from the constant noise of her little ones, made a sanctuary for herself in the simplest way. "I threw my apron over my head," she said, "and there is my closet."[15]

A Quiet Hour

For most of us, it may be harder to find a quiet hour. I don't mean an hour as in sixty minutes exactly, but a portion of time away from the engagements of the day, the intrusions of business or pleasure, and dedicated to God. Men from times gone by may have stayed out in the fields in meditation before God until darkness wrapped around them. But for us who live with the clang of machinery and the roar of traffic always in our ears, whose crowding obligations jostle against each other as the hours fly by, are often tempted to use those moments of solitude and quiet for ourselves rather than spending them in sacred communion with heaven.

Dr. Dale says somewhere that if each day had forty-eight hours, and every week had fourteen days, we might actually get through our work, but with the way things are, it's impossible. There is at least an edge of truth in this amusing statement. If we are to have a quiet hour in the middle of our busy duties and keep it sacred, we will have to think ahead and deny ourselves. We must be prepared to skip many things that are pleasant, and some things that are profitable to us.[16] We will have to find the time. We might have to take it from our recreation time, from social interaction, from study, or from good works, if we are to find time every day to go into a room, shut the door, and pray to our Father who is in secret.[17]

Some of us, in all honesty and sincerity, will just accept that we are unable to do more than we think is possible. Some of us will say, "I know that I don't spend much time alone in a room praying, but I try to keep the habit of continual prayer."

It's even thought that this means more and is better than spending time alone, quietly. The two things should not be compared as if one is greater or more beneficial. Each one is necessary for a balanced Christian life, and each one was perfectly maintained in the life of Jesus. He was always embraced in the Divine love; His communion with the Father was constant; He was the Son of Man who is in heaven.

THE BIBLE TELLS us in Luke 5:16 that it was a habit of His to go off by Himself into the wilderness and pray. Dean Vaughan comments on it this way: "It was not one withdrawal, nor one wilderness, nor one prayer, it happened many times—the withdrawals were repeated; the wildernesses were more than one, the prayers were habitual." Crowds were thronging and pressing Him; great multitudes came together to hear and to be healed of their sicknesses, and He had no time to even eat. But He found time to pray.

The one who always looked to find time to be alone was the Son of God, even though He had no sin to confess, no weakness to regret, no doubts to conquer, no lack of love to overcome. We also shouldn't think that His prayers were just peaceful meditations or delightful times of communion. They were exhausting and aggressive, from the time in the wilderness when angels came to minister to the Man of Sorrows bowing down, right up to that awful agony where His sweat was like great drops of blood. His prayers were sacrifices, offered up with strong crying and tears.

Now, if it was part of the Son of God's sacred discipline to have frequent times of being on His own to pray, how much more for us, broken as we are and disabled by so much sin, to be diligent in the exercise of private prayer!

To rush through this duty would be robbing ourselves of the benefits that come from it. Of course, we know that prayer cannot be measured by divisions of time, but the advantages that we gain from secret prayer cannot be obtained unless we deliberately enter in with some thought and planning beforehand. We must "shut the door," close off everything and make sure there is enough amount of time to accomplish and fulfill the commitment before us.

In the morning, we should look forward to the duties of the day, anticipating those situations in which temptation may lurk, and preparing ourselves to embrace such opportunities of usefulness that may be offered to us. In the evening, we should comment on the good things that have happened, consider whether we achieved holiness, and try to profit from the lessons God wants us to learn. And we must always acknowledge and reject sin. Then there are the numerous items to pray for: The well-being and growth of the church, the conversion and sanctification of our friends and family, the advance of missionaries and their efforts, and the coming of the kingdom of Christ.

All this cannot be squashed into a few crowded moments. We must not be rushed when we enter the secret place. Once, Hudson Taylor was so fully occupied during the day with managing the demands of the China Inland Mission that he found it difficult to find the necessary freedom for private prayer. As a result, he made himself a rule to rise each morning at two o'clock, pray until four, then lie down to sleep until he had to wake up for the day.

In the Jewish Church, it was customary to set apart some time for meditation and prayer three times a day—in the morning, at noon, and in the evening (Psalm 55:17; Dan. 6:10). But in the Biblical region of the Middle East, it is very hot and there is a natural pause to activities at midday that does not occur in places with cooler climates. Where it is possible to take a few moments in the middle of the day's duties, it should definitely be done.[18]

Nature even teaches us that morning and evening are suitable occasions when we can approach God. A question that has been frequently discussed, and is not without interest, is: Should we use the morning or the evening for our more deliberate and extended times of waiting on God? Each person can answer this question for himself or herself depending on their situation. But it should always be understood that we give our best to God.

A Quiet Heart

For most of us, perhaps, it is most difficult to acquire a quiet heart. In the Middle Ages, a group devoted to spending time with God desired to present themselves before Him in silence, that He might teach them what they should say and what their hearts should expect. Stephen Gurnall acknowledges that it is far more difficult to hang up the big bell than it is to ring it when it has been hung. Robert Murray Mc'Cheyne, the Scottish minister, used to say that much of his prayer time was spent in preparing to pray.[19]

A New England Puritan writes: "While I was at the Word, I saw I had a wild heart, which was as hard to stand and abide before the presence of God in an ordinance, as a bird before any man." And John Bunyan says of his own deep experience: "Oh! the loopholes that the heart has in the time of prayer; none knows how many detours the heart has and back-lanes to slip away from the presence of God."[20]

There are three great, but simple acts of faith, which will help us to keep our minds focused on God.

1. Firstly, let us recognize our acceptance before God through the death of the Lord Jesus. Traditionally, when a traveler from one of the more orthodox churches arrives in Jerusalem, the first thing he would do, before looking for refreshment or rest, is to visit the traditional scene of Jesus' crucifixion. Our first act in prayer should be to surrender our hearts to the power of the blood of Christ. It was in the power of the ritual sacrifice that the high priest in Israel passed through the veil on the day of atonement. It is in the power of the accepted offering of the Lamb that we are privileged to come into the presence of God.

"Therefore, brothers, since we have confidence to enter the holy places by the blood of Jesus, by the new and living way that he opened for us through the curtain, that is, through his flesh, and since we have a great priest over the house of God, let us draw near with a true heart in full assurance of faith, with our hearts sprinkled clean from an evil conscience and our bodies washed with pure water. Let us hold fast the

confession of our hope without wavering, for he who promised is faithful" (Heb. 10:19-23).

"*Were I with the trespass laden Of a thousand worlds beside,*

Yet by that path I enter—The blood of the Lamb who died."

1. It is important that we also confess and receive the grace of the Spirit, for there is nothing holy and nothing good without Him. He teaches us to cry, "Abba, Father," searches the deep things of God for us, reveals the mind and will of Christ to us, helps our weaknesses and intercedes on our behalf according to God.[21] "*And we all, with unveiled face, beholding the glory of the Lord, are being transformed into the same image from one degree of glory to another. For this comes from the Lord who is the Spirit*" (2 Cor. 3:18).

When we enter the inner chamber, we should present ourselves before God in humility and trust, and open our hearts to being filled with the Holy Spirit. So, we will receive from the praying Spirit and commit to the praying Christ, those requests that are of God, and express themselves, through our human hearts and sinful lips, "*with groanings too deep for words*" (Rom 8:26).

Without the support of the Holy Spirit, prayer becomes a difficult chore. Somebody who prayed often said, "As for my heart, when I go to pray, I find it hates to go to God, and when it is with Him, hates to stay with Him, that many times I am forced in my prayers, first to beg of God that He would take my heart, and set it on Himself in Christ, and when it is there, that He would keep it there. Many times I don't know what to pray for, I am so blind, nor how to pray, I am so ignorant; only the Spirit helps our infirmities."

1. A Puritan once stated that "the Spirit rides most triumphantly in His own chariot." If the Holy Spirit chooses the Bible as His way to enlighten, comfort, arouse, and rebuke us, then it will be good for us at the beginning of our prayers to direct our hearts towards the Scriptures. This will really help to calm our conflicting minds if we open the Bible and read it as though we are in the presence of God until He speaks to us through the verses that we read.

George Muller confessed that often, he could not pray until he had steadied his mind upon a verse or chapter.[22] Is it not God's prerogative to break the silence? *"You have said, "Seek my face. My heart says to you, Your face, Lord, do I seek"* (Psalm 27:8). Is it not appropriate that His will should order all the acts of our prayer with Himself? Let us be silent before God, that He may shape and mold us.

"So shall I keep forever in my heart one silent space; A little sacred spot of loneliness, Where to set up the memory of Thy Cross, A little quiet garden, where no man

May pass or rest forever, sacred to visions of Thy sorrow and Thy love."

Study Guide

McIntyre's approach to prayer is not just quoting verses and listing examples of people, but he uses a practical and very simple outline for us to follow. In this, it is easy to look at the three requirements, or as he calls them, the equipment that is needed to enter the secret place for ourselves, and see if they are present in our own prayer lives or not.

In working through the questions, it is a good exercise to keep a notebook and pen close by to keep a record of your thoughts, answers, and admissions of where you are personally. It will also help to look back at your entries once you have finished reading this book, or even a few months later, and see how you have progressed in your prayer life.

1. Matthew 6:6 is a key verse in this book as it summarizes what McIntyre is trying to say in a very practical and straightforward way. Read it as an instruction. How do you compare in terms of fulfilling its directions?
2. Do you have a quiet place that you go to in order to pray? What alternative do you have?
3. Do you think it's possible that "the heart that turns to God can find quiet," even when it's busy and noisy at work or at home?
4. If you are honest, how much time do you spend praying each day or each week? Be bold enough to write this figure down in your notes.
5. Look at the comment: "I know that I don't spend much time alone in a room praying, but I try to keep

the habit of continual prayer." What do you understand about this? How does McIntyre respond to such a statement?
6. Why is finding a quiet heart the most difficult item on this list?
7. Of the three acts of faith that will keep us focused on God and reaching a place of having a quiet heart, which do you find easy, and which ones do you struggle with?

3
THE DIRECTION OF THE MIND

"You should go to prayer, that you may deliver yourself wholly into the hands of God, with perfect resignation, exerting an act of faith, believing that you are in the Divine Presence, afterward settling in that holy rest, with quietness, silence, and tranquility; and endeavoring for a whole day, a whole year, and your whole life, to continue that first act of contemplation, by faith and love."
–Molinos.

"Satan strikes either at the root of faith or at the root of diligence."
–John Livingstone.

"The sum is: Remember always the presence of God; rejoice always in the will of God and direct all to the glory of God."
–Archbishop Leighton.

In Essex, in the year 1550, a number of believers who had received the Word of God as their only rule of faith and conduct differed on certain issues with the dominant party in the church, and they met to discuss the order of worship. The main point in the debate related to the attitude one should have in prayer—whether it was better to stand or kneel, to have the head covered or uncovered. The decision they arrived at was that the real question had little to do with bodily posture but the direction of the mind. It was agreed that the proper attitude was the one that expressed the desires and emotions of the heart the best.

Jesus' words that he spoke to His disciples in Matthew 6:6 indicate clearly the attitude of spirit we need in our approach to God.

Realize the Presence of God

Firstly, it's necessary to realize the presence of God.[23] The One who fills earth and heaven 'is,' in a singular and impressive sense, in the secret place. As the electric current in the atmosphere is concentrated in a lightning flash, so the presence of God becomes vivid and powerful in the prayer room. Bishop Jeremy Taylor backs this idea up by stating: "At the beginning of acting on your belief, make an act of adoration; that is, solemnly worship God, and place yourself in His presence, and see Him with the eye of faith; and let your desires fix on Him as the object of your worship, and the reason of your hope, and the fountain of your blessing. For when you have placed yourself before Him, and kneel in His presence, it is likely that all the other aspects of your devotion will be made clear by the wisdom of such an awareness, and the glory of such a presence."

Our Father 'is' in the secret place. Then we shall find Him in a 'recollected' spirit, in the quiet of a heart that fears His name. The dew falls the most when there is no wind at night. The massive tides of the ocean lift themselves without foaming or crashing. The person who prays with a true direction of spirit, "Our Father, who is in heaven," is often taken up into heaven before he is even aware of it happening. "But, oh how rare it is!" cries Francois Fnelon, "How rare it is to find a soul quiet enough to hear God speak!"

So many of us have untrained ears. We are like the Indian hunters who can hear the crackle of a twig far off in the dim forest but are deaf to the thunder of Niagara only a short distance away. Brother Lawrence, who lived to practice the presence of God, puts it this way: "As for my set hours of prayer, they are only a continuation of the same exercise. Sometimes I consider myself there as a stone before a carver, ready for him to make a statue of me; presenting myself before God I desire Him to form His perfect image in my soul and make me entirely like Himself. At other times, when I apply myself to prayer, I feel all my spirit and all my soul lift itself up without any care or effort of mine, and it continues as it was suspended and firmly fixed in God, as in its center and place of rest."

The realization of the Divine presence is the firm state of our spirit in the right attitude in private prayer.

John Spilsbury of Bromsgrove, who was put in Worcester jail for testifying about Jesus, said this: "I shall not fear a prison anymore as I did, because I had so much of my Heavenly Father's company that it became a palace to me." Another person in a similar position said: "I thought of Jesus until every stone in my cell shone like a ruby." For us, in our lives, the dull room in which we talk with God, as a person speaks to their friend, can light up like a sapphire and a sardius stone, and be like Moses' opening in the rock on Sinai where God's glory was seen, until he couldn't look at it anymore, and his face shone like fire.

Our realization of the presence of God may come with little or no emotion at all. Our spirits may be as though they are dead under God's hand, with no delight or sense of anything spiritual. But we shouldn't become lazy in our prayer as a result. Instead of pulling back at these times, we should double our efforts. The prayer that goes up to God in dark or dry periods will bring such a blessing to us, even more than what we have received in easier, more fulfilling times. The prayer which rises from a place of hardship may have an abundant and glorious return. At the same time, we are also privileged to have seasons when the winds of God blow freely from His throne of grace, and the breath of spring stirs in the King's gardens.

The old Scottish preachers used to talk much about gaining access. A story is told of Robert Bruce who had two visitors on a certain morning. He said to them, "You must go and leave me for some time. I thought last night when I lay down I had a good measure of the Lord's presence, and now I have wrestled for an hour or two, and have not yet got access." Maybe in his time of solitude, there was a disproportionate subjectivity, but his desire was surely commendable.

What good does it do for us to stay in Jerusalem if we do not see the King's face? And when He comes out of His royal chambers with His blessings, do we wait for Him to offer our worship and service? Jonathan Edwards resolved that whenever he would find himself "in a good frame for divine contemplation," he wouldn't even allow lunchtime to interrupt his engagement with His Lord. "I will forgo my dinner," he said, "rather than be broken off." When the fire of God shone on Carmel, it was Ahab who went down to eat and drink; it was Elijah who went up to pray.

Honesty in Prayer

He who 'is' in the secret place sees in secret, and we need to be honest when we kneel in His presence.

When we address God, we like to speak of Him in a way we think we should speak, and there are times when we don't have enough words for what we are actually feeling. But it is best that we should be perfectly honest and sincere with Him. He will allow us to say anything we need to, as long as we say as though we are speaking to God. "*I say to God, my rock,*" exclaims the psalmist, "*Why have you forgotten me?*" (Psa. 42:9). If he had said, "Lord, You can't forget: isn't my name written on the palms of Your hands?" he would have spoken more worthily, but less truly.

On one occasion, Jeremiah failed to interpret God correctly. He cried, as if he was angry, "*O Lord, you have deceived me, and I was deceived; you are stronger than I, and you have prevailed*" (Jer. 20:7). These are terrible words to say before Him who never changes, is always truthful and faithful. But the prophet spoke as the way he felt, and the Lord not only pardoned him, He met and blessed him there.

It's possible that you may even have a complaint against God; a long-standing contentious issue has come between your heart and His grace. If you were to say what you really wanted to, you would say to him, "Why have You done this to me, in this way?" Then dare to say, with reverence and boldness, all that is in your heart. "*Set forth your case, says the Lord; bring your proofs, says the King of Jacob*" (Isa. 41.21). Bring your grievance into the light of His face; make your complaint clear and known. Then listen to His answer, because in gentleness and truth, He will clear Himself of the charge of unkindness that you bring against Him. And in His light, you will see light.

But remember that this is a private matter between you and God, and you must not insult or speak badly of Him to anyone. "*If I had said, 'I will speak thus,' I would have betrayed the generation of your children*" (Psa. 73:15). John Livingstone of Ancrum, in a day of darkness, made a very excellent resolution: "Finding myself deserted, as I thought I was, and not being met in my particular state, I made a promise to God not to tell it to anyone but Him so that I should complain or foster misbelief in myself or others."

But there is another area in prayer where we need to be honest. There have been times in each of our lives when the Spirit of God has given us more love and desire. Our prayers rose straight up to heaven, and were about to present themselves before the throne when we suddenly remembered something that had to be taken care of, some harmful indulgence we had tolerated or sin not yet repented of. This happened in order that we might give up and deny those evil desires and actions, and follow that which is good. This is why the Holy Spirit gave us His assistance in prayer.[24] It was His intention that at that time, we would be reminded and given the strength to purify ourselves from every stain and live as being purchased of God.

But maybe, instead of accepting His assistance, we turned from the light, away from the guidance of God. Then we could no longer see God and the Holy Spirit, who helps us in our times of weakness, withdrew because He was grieved. We can probably trace our lack of effective time in prayer back to this moment.

- "*If I had cherished iniquity in my heart, the Lord would not have listened*" (Psalm 66:18).
- "*If one turns away his ear from hearing the law, even his prayer is an abomination*" (Prov. 28:9).
- "*Your iniquities have made a separation between you and your God, and your sins have hidden his face from you so that he does not hear*" (Isa. 59:2).
- "*When you spread out your hands, I will hide my eyes from you; even though you make many prayers, I will not listen*" (Isa. 1:15).

In sending messages in morse code or telegraph, if the receiver is not in tune with the transmitter, communication is impossible. In true prayer, God and the person praying must be united in agreement. Jean Cavalier, a Huguenot leader, who had lived for years enjoying a steady and continuous relationship with God, was deceived by his pride and vanity and gave up the cause to which he had devoted his life. Finally, he came to England and joined the British army. When he met Queen Anne, she said, "Does God visit you now, Monsieur Cavalier?" The young man bowed his head and was silent.

Christmas Evans tells of a time when he lost his faith; a time of powerlessness and failure followed. But the Lord visited him in mercy. *"Now when Jesus came, he found that Lazarus had already been in the tomb four days"* (John 11:17). Immediately, he began to beg that the passion and joy he'd had in years before might be restored. "On the Caerphilly Mountain," he related, "the spirit of prayer fell on me as it had once in Anglesea. I wept and cried out, and gave myself to Christ. I wept long and begged Jesus Christ, and my heart poured out its requests before Him on the mountain." Then a period of marvelous blessing followed.

On the other hand, *"If our heart does not condemn us, we have confidence before God; and whatever we ask we receive from him, because we keep his commandments and do what pleases him"* (I John 3:21-22).

The devotional writers of the Middle Ages were used to distinguishing between a pure intention and a right intention. According to them, the former was the fruit of sanctification; the latter was the condition of sanctification. The pure intention implied a trained and disciplined will; the right intention is a will humbly surrendered at the Master's feet. Now, what God requires from those who seek His face is a right intention—a deliberate, surrendered, and joyful acceptance of His good and perfect will. All true prayer must fall back upon the great atonement, in which the Man of Sorrows put into action, the prayer of His agony, "*My Father, if it be possible, let this cup pass from me; nevertheless, not as I will, but as you will*" (Matt. 26:39). He has transmitted to us His own prayer: We offer it in the power of His sacrifice. "*When you pray, say: Father...Your kingdom come*" (Luke 11:2).

Lord, here I am holding this will of mine in my trembling hands—a thing which seems small. Only You, Jesus, can understand that when I surrender this to You, I surrender my all. It's drenched with tears and stained with sighs, held in my grasp until there is no beauty left. Now, before Your throne where it lies, my prayer ascends, "Let Your will be done."

Faith

It is necessary that when we draw near to God, we should come in faith:

- "Pray to your Father" (Matt 6:6).
- "*When you pray, say: 'Father'*" (Luke 11:2).
- "*Fear not, little flock, for it is your Father's good pleasure to give you the kingdom*" (Luke 12:32).
- "*Your Father knows what you need*" (Matt. 6:8).
- "*The Father Himself loves you*" (John 16:27).

The whole philosophy of prayer is contained in words like these. "This word 'Father,'" writes Luther, "has overcome God."

1. It must be said that with God, no miracle is impossible. It must be acknowledged that He rewards those that diligently seek Him, and every true prayer will be blessed. But faith in God is not a light or trivial thing. Robert Bruce of Edinburgh used to sometimes pause in his preaching, and then lean over the pulpit and very seriously say, "I think it's a great matter to believe there is a God." Once he confessed that during three years he had never said, "My God," without being "challenged and unsettled."

"These words, 'My God,'" said Ebenezer Erskine, "are the marrow of the Gospel." To be able to hold the living God within our feeble grasp, and say with assurance, "*God, our God, shall bless us*" (Psalm 67:6), demands a faith that is not naturally in us from birth.

But it is comforting to remember that even a weak faith will succeed to overcome. "Is it not a wonder," says Robert Blair, "that our words in prayer, which almost die as they come out of our lips, should climb so well and go into heaven?" It's definitely a wonder, but all the doings of God in grace are wonderful. Like the miner, whose trained eye detects the glitter of the precious metal embedded in small flakes through the coarse grain of the rocks, God observes the rare but costly faith that lies immersed in our unbelief.

Standing somewhere on the slopes of Mount Hermon, Jesus said to His disciples, "*If you have faith like a grain of mustard seed, you will say to this mountain, 'Move from here to there,' and it will move, and nothing will be impossible for you*" (Matt. 17:20). The mountain that the word of faith would lift up and throw into the sea was the immeasurable mass dominating the horizon to the north of Palestine, whose roots run under the whole land of Emmanuel, and whose dew refreshed the city of God.

"Faith, mighty faith, the promise sees, And looks to that alone;

Laughs at impossibilities, And cries, It shall be done."

WHEN THE PILGRIMS, in Bunyan's *Pilgrim's Progress*, came to the Delectable Mountains, the shepherds showed them a man standing on Mount Marvel who *"tumbled the hills about with words."* That man was the son of Mr. Great Grace, the King's champion, and he was set there *"to teach pilgrims to believe through, or to tumble out of their ways whatever difficulties they should meet, by faith."*

1. But this God who is ours is our Father. Our Lord gives us His own rights and privileges. He gives us the key that unlocks all the doors of the treasury of God. *"For all the promises of God find their Yes in him. That is why it is through him that we utter our Amen to God for his glory"* (2 Cor. 1:20). In Him, we draw near to God. In Him, we ask our requests with confidence.

Ralph Erskine tells us that, on a certain Sabbath evening, he had unusual freedom in prayer through the name of the Lord Jesus; "I was helped to pray in secret with an outpouring of the soul before the Lord, owning my claim to the promise, my claim to pardon, my claim to grace, my claim to daily bread, my claim to a comfortable life, my claim to a stingless death, my claim to a glorious resurrection, and my claim to everlasting life and happiness: to be, only, only in Christ, and in God through Him as a promising God."

When we pray to our Father, we offer our prayers in the name of Jesus with His authority. We must not think, however, that the name of Jesus may be used by us as we like. God cannot wisely deal with His children the same way that Ahasuerus dealt with Mordecai when he gave him the great seal and said, "*But you may write as you please with regard to the Jews, in the name of the king, and seal it with the king's ring, for an edict written in the name of the king and sealed with the king's ring cannot be revoked*" (Esther 8:8).

John Bunyan shows his usual spiritual discernment when, in his *Holy War*, he discusses the requests that the men of Mansoul sent to Emmanuel, and He did not answer. After a while, "they agreed together to write another petition and to send it away to Emmanuel for relief. But Mr. Godly-Fear stood up and answered that he knew his Lord, the Prince, never did, nor ever would, receive a petition for these matters from the hand of any unless the Lord Secretary's signed it. 'And this,' he quoted, 'is the reason you did not succeed so far.' Then they said they would write one, and get the Lord Secretary's to sign it. But Mr. Godly-Fear answered again that he knew also that the Lord Secretary would not sign any petition that He had not a hand in composing and drawing up."[25]

The prayer of faith is a middle term between the intercession of the Holy Spirit and the intercession of Christ.[26] It is the divinely appointed way that the wordless groanings of the Spirit, who lives inside His people as in a temple, are conveyed and committed to the Mediator, who "*lives to make intercession for them*" (Heb 7:25). And so in a strange and special method, those who speak of Jesus are given the privilege to become workers together with God.

Study Guide

Our minds are often our worst enemies! They are always busy, especially in times of prayer. The distracting thoughts, ideas, and plans that we make while we should be spending time with God don't help at all.

McIntyre's real approach to prayer is to acknowledge these human struggles and give us some very clear instructions to deal with them. Rather than writing a book that sets the spiritual bar so far and out of reach, he brings it down to our everyday level by dealing with the issue.

By being honest and real with ourselves, we can answer and work through these questions. If you are vulnerable enough to admit your shortcomings to others you can trust, then being held accountable for what you are working through is a huge step forward.

1. What do you understand by the term, 'the presence of God?' Look at these verses and see if this lines up: James 4:10, Acts 3:19, Psalm 51:11, 2 Thess. 1:9.
2. Again, a quiet heart is mentioned as necessary for someone to find or enter God's presence. Why is this more important than the way you sit, stand, or lie down in prayer?

3. McIntyre makes this beautiful statement: "What good does it do for us to stay in Jerusalem if we do not see the King's face?" What do you understand about this?
4. There are two types of honesty in prayer spoken about here. What are they? Have you ever been this genuine and open before God?
5. What is the difference between a "pure intention and a right intention?"
6. Read Hebrews 11:1. What is your understanding of faith? Why is it so important to have faith when we enter into prayer?
7. Explain the meaning of faith as a middle term between the intercession of the Holy Spirit and Jesus.

4

THE ENGAGEMENT—WORSHIP

*"We praise Thee...We give thanks to Thee for Thy great glory,
O Lord God."*
–Book of Common Prayer.

*"Were there nothing else
For which to praise the heavens but only love,
That only love was cause enough for praise."*
–Tennyson.

*"Praise Him, ever praise Him,
For remembering the dust of earth."*
–Morgan Rhys.

"*Go into your room and shut the door and <u>pray</u>*" (Matt 6:6). The word here, the one that is most frequently used in the New Testament to describe prayer, implies a desire towards; and while it suggests petition, it is general enough to include the whole of our engagement in the secret place—Worship, Confession, Request. In this chapter, we shall speak of the first of these—Worship.

When Scipio Africanus entered Rome, after he had conquered the proud city of Carthage, he rode in procession along the Way of Triumph, swept over the slope of the Velia, passed reverently down the ancient Way of Sacrifice, then climbed the long ascent of the Capitol, scattering with both his hands, gifts to the people, while the air was torn with the applause of the crowd. Amid the rejoicing multitudes, there were probably some whose most obvious feeling of gratitude was because of the generosity of the conqueror in his triumphant hour. Others cheered the end to the years of terror they suffered and thought emotionally of the fair fields of Italy, now freed from the control of a foreigner. While others, forgetting about their personal benefits or national enlargement for a moment, praised the personal qualities of Scipio Africanus—his resourcefulness, his kindness, his courage, his courtesy.

In the same way, the tribute of praise that Christians are instructed to give to the Lord may come from the acknowledgment of daily mercy, thanksgiving for the great redemption, or contemplation of godly perfection.

Acknowledgment of Daily Mercy

"Memory," says Aristotle, "is the scribe of the soul." Let memory bring her pen and paper, and write. Fraser of Brea, once a prisoner on the Bass Rock because of his stand for Jesus, decided to look for and record the loving kindnesses of God. He did so with joy in his heart. He says, "The reminding and meditating on the Lord's dealings with me as to soul and body, His many mercies, has been very good for me, cleared my case, confirmed my heart of God's love and my interest in Him, and made me love Him. Oh,...what wells of water my eyes have opened to see, which before were hidden. Hardly anything else has done more good for me than this."

Let us take the trouble to observe and consider the Lord's dealings with us, and we will definitely find encouraging reminders of His kindness and truth. His mercies are new every morning. He makes the departing night rejoice. His thoughts concerning us are as many as the sands on the shore, and they are all thoughts of peace. Those blessings that happen so often that they seem common and ordinary, finding their way into our simple daily lives like golden threads, should be fondly remembered. For they are often incredibly great. "I have experienced today the most exquisite pleasure that I have ever had in my life," said a young patient in bed; "I was able to breathe freely for about five minutes."

In Dr. Judson's house in Burma, some friends were talking about the highest form of happiness which could come from circumstances happening around them, and each person backed up their own opinion by quoting other people's great viewpoints. "No," said Dr. Judson, who had been recalling his terrible imprisonment in Ava, "these men were not qualified to judge. What do you think of floating down the Irrawadi, on a cool, moonlight evening, with your wife by your side, and your baby in your arms, free, all free? But you cannot understand it either; it needs twenty-one months' qualification, and I can scarcely regret my twenty-one months of misery when I recall that one delicious thrill. I think I have had a better appreciation of what heaven may be since then." But how often do we thank God just for the joy of simply living freely and being able to have healthy bodies?

"The river past, and God forgotten," is an English proverb that should never apply to those who have tasted that the Lord is gracious. *"Praise befits the upright"* (Psalm 33:1) is the command of the Old Testament. *"Give thanks in all circumstances"* (1 Thess. 5:18) is the decision of the New Testament.

Even a non-Christian once said, "What can I, a lame old man, do but sing His praise, and exhort others to do the same?"[27] For the beauty of nature, the fellowship of the good, the tender love of home; for safe conduct in temptation, strength to overcome, deliverance from evil; for the generosity, the patience, the sympathy of God; and for ten thousand unseen or forgotten mercies, let us never grow tired of blessing His Holy Name. *"Give thanks to the Lord, for he is good, for his steadfast love endures forever"* (Psalm 136:1).[28]

But if things become difficult for us, and hardships make everything seem dark, are we still to give thanks, and bless God? Definitely.

"Trials make the promise sweet;

Trials give new life to prayer;

Trials bring me to His feet,

Lay me low, and keep me there."

LET us thank God for our trials. We live in a land of restriction. But, like Immanuel Kant's garden, it is "endlessly high." The air is fresh, and the sun is clear. The winter is frosty but kind. With the springtime comes the singing of birds, and the bloom and fragrance of flowers. And if, even in the summer, there is "a cool and strong breeze," there is always the smile of God.

On the other hand, Augustine's words are true; "Earthly riches are full of poverty." Pantries filled with food and drink will never satisfy a hungry heart. Rich, fine clothes can only cover a poor life. The loud music of fame cannot silence the conflict of the spirit. The best night that Jacob ever spent was when he had a stone for his pillow and the evening skies as his tent. When Job was mocked by children whose fathers he wouldn't have trusted to look after his sheepdogs, he was made a spectacle to angels and became the theme of their wonder and joy. The defeat which Adam endured in Paradise, Jesus overcame in the desolation of the desert and the anguish of His passion. The cross we are called to bear may be heavy, but we don't have to carry it far. And when God allows us to lay it down, then heaven begins.

Chrysostom, on his way to exile, exclaimed, "Thank God for everything."

If we imitate these people, we shall never have a bad day. Alexander Simson, a famous Scottish minister many years ago, fell and broke his leg while he was out walking. Someone found him "sitting with his broken leg in his arm, and crying out, 'Blessed be the Lord; blessed be His name.'" He saw that all things work together for good to those who love God, and so he was wise. Richard Baxter found a reason to bless God for having to endure thirty-five years of pain. And Samuel Rutherford exclaims, "Oh, what I owe to the furnace, the file, and the hammer of my Lord Jesus!"

Thanksgiving for Redemption

But even looking at all the mercies given to us by God should bring us to think of our acceptance in Christ. The river of the water of life, which makes the desert bloom, flows from the throne of God and the Lamb. The benefits of that gracious, steadfast covenant are for our use and pleasure by the seal of Jesus' blood.

"There's not a gift His hand bestows,

But cost His heart a groan."

THERE MAY BE no water in the bottle, but the Well of the Covenant is like a fresh spring so close that we can even hear the music of its flow. Thieves may steal our money, but our treasure is in the safe of our hearts. God may take away things that are precious to us, but has He not given us Jesus? And no matter how the prayer of thanksgiving drifts through the gracious gifts of God, it will inevitably come to rest at the feet of the Lord.

But praising Jesus is not something small or trivial. What Thomas Boston says about preaching is also true about praising: "I saw the preaching of Christ to be the most difficult thing; for that, though the whole world is full of wonders, yet here are depths beyond all." And so he maintained this manner before God for a long time, "that he might see Christ by a spiritual illumination." He was so eager for his prayer to be heard and accepted, and so hurt that his heart knew nothing of Christ, that his physical health began to be affected. But, there were times when his heart went out in love to Jesus, seeking Him, that he found his contentment and delight in Him.

The Passover in Israel was celebrated on the evening of the great deliverance, which then became a night that must be observed before the Lord. Let us often remember our salvation from a bondage that was more bitter than the one they suffered in Egypt.

John Bunyan has this beneficial advice: "Remember the days and years of times gone by. Remember also your songs in the night, and speak with your own hearts. Yes, look diligently, and leave no corner of your heart unsearched, for that treasure hid, even the treasure of your first and second experience of God's grace towards you. Remember the word that first took hold of you. Remember the fear of your conscience and of death and hell. Remember also your tears and prayers to God—how you cried out for mercy! Have you not got a place of suffering like Mount Mizar to remember? Have you forgotten the room, the closet, the stable, the barn, and other such places, where God visited your hearts? Remember also the word—the word on which the Lord caused you to hope."

It's also good for us to look into the riches and glory of the inheritance that God has invited us to share in. The blood of Jesus, the grace of the Spirit, the light of God's face, are "three jewels worth more than heaven. In the name of Christ, there are ten thousand treasures of joy."[29] Perhaps the most acceptable form of worship and the quickest motivation to praise, when we recall the mercies which are made sure to us in the blood of an eternal covenant," is the act of appropriation by which we become heirs to the purchased possession that is ours in Christ.

Dr. Chalmers was one of those who discovered this open secret. In his diary, we find many expressions such as these:

- "Began my first waking minutes with a confident hold of Christ as my Savior. A day of great quietness."
- "Let the taking hold of Christ as my propitiation be the constant first act of every morning."
- "Began the day with a distinct act of confidence, but should renew it through the day."
- "Began again with an act of confidence; but why not a continuous confidence in the Savior?"
- "I have returned more often to the acts of faith in Christ, and I can have no doubt of this being the habit that is to bring me right."
- "Returning to the topic of a large confidence and belief in the promises of the Gospel, let me act on the command, "Open your mouth wide, and I will fill it."

It's also our satisfying duty to remember with thanksgiving how Jesus has led us. Otto Funcke's brief autobiography is beautifully titled *The Footprints of God in the Pathway of My Life*. The way of God's direction may lead from the bitter waters of Marah to the cooler shade of Elim's palms. It may pass through the fiery desert, but it reaches on towards the Mount of God. It may descend to the valley of the shadow of death, but it will bring us out and through to the pleasant land of the promises of God—"A land of corn and wine and oil, favored with God's peculiar smile, with every blessing."

And in that right way, there is always the comforting and captivating presence of our God and Savior. We can't recall the mercies and not remember Him. With His hand that was pierced, He took the bitter cup and drank from it until His lips were wet with our sorrow and doom. And now the cup of bitterness has become sweet. Where His footsteps fell, the wilderness rejoiced, and the desolate places of our life became as fruitful as Mount Carmel. A rugged track beneath our feet ran into the dark night, but the tender love of His presence was like a lamp to our feet and a light on our path.

His name is fragrance, His voice is music, His countenance is health. Dr. Judson, during his last period of illness, had a wonderful period in praise. He would suddenly exclaim, as the tears ran down his face, "Oh, the love of Christ, the love of Christ! We cannot understand it now, but what a beautiful study for eternity." Again and again, though his pain was constant and severe, he would cry in holy ecstasy, "Oh, the love of Christ, the love of Christ!"

Such praises rise up in their tune until they harmonize with the glory of the new song that fills the heavens, *"Worthy are you to take the scroll and to open its seals, for you were slain, and by your blood, you ransomed people for God from every tribe and language and people and nation, and you have made them a kingdom and priests to our God, and they shall reign on the earth"* (Rev. 5:9-10).

Contemplation of Godly Perfection

And so, praise addressed to God in the name and memory of Jesus inevitably becomes adoration. Often, this praise is silent. Isaiah, transported by faith into the inner sanctuary, was swept up in the worship of the seraphim, and joined in spirit in the never-ending adoration of the Triune God —*"Holy, holy, holy is the Lord of hosts; the whole earth is full of his glory!"* (Isa. 6:3). The angels poured their heavenly song down onto the fields of Bethlehem, *"Glory to God in the highest;"* (Luke 2:14) and our sad earth heard, and was comforted.

"Angels, help us to adore Him; You behold Him face to face!"

But even these bright intelligences are unable to show all the praise He is worthy of.[30]

There are reports that John Janeway, when he was deep in prayer, hardly knew whether he was "in the body, or out of the body." Tersteegen said to some friends who had gathered around him, "I sit here and talk with you, but inside me is eternal adoration, unceasing and undisturbed." Woodrow relates that on one occasion, Mr. Carstairs was invited to take part in communion services at Calder, near Glasgow. He was wonderfully assisted and had a strange outpouring throughout the whole sermon. Those who heard him were unusually affected, and glory seemed to fill the house. "A Christian man that had been at the table, and had to leave the church, when he tried to get in again, could not succeed for some time, but stood outside the door, filled with the thoughts of the glory that was in the house, for nearly half-an-hour, and could think of nothing else."

Dr. A. J. Gordon describes his impression of a dialogue he had with Joseph Rabinowitz, whom Dr. Delitzsch considered the most remarkable Jewish convert since Saul of Tarsus: "We will not forget the radiance that would come into his face as he expounded the Messianic psalms at our morning or evening worship, and how, as here and there he caught a glimpse of the suffering or glorified Christ, he would suddenly lift his hands and his eyes to heaven in a burst of admiration, exclaiming with Thomas, after he had seen the nail-prints, 'My Lord, and my God!'"

For many of us, emotions may be weak, and experiences of spiritual ecstasy may be rare. Our love for Christ may express itself more naturally in the right conduct than in a flood of praise. But it is possible that for each Christian there are seasons of communion when, as we turn to the invisible glory, the veil of sense fades away, and we see the face of Him who died for our sins, who rose for our justification, who now waits for us at the right hand of God. But, we must never forget that adoration does not exhaust itself in pleasing our emotions, but it turns us to say: "*Our Father in heaven, hallowed be your name*" (Matt. 6:9).

Study Guide

Again, McIntyre provides us with a clear-cut guide for prayer by dividing it into three sections, although these should not be taken as the only approach to take or a rigid pattern we must follow. The Holy Spirit can move and guide as He chooses, and we should be free to follow His direction. But for us, trying to make sense of spending time with God, they are clear signposts that can help us find our way to a more stimulating habit of prayer.

If you have questions that arise from the passages or the study questions, be free to share these with someone else. It's always good to find answers or help from a person you trust or you see as wise in spiritual matters—an elder, pastor, counselor. It's also good to hear a different viewpoint and engage in a healthy discussion on such matters.

1. Why does McIntyre think it's important to begin with remembering God's mercies in our lives?
2. Read Thess 5:18. How do you compare in this regard? Are you someone who is always grateful to God—in every circumstance?
3. What do you understand by Romans 12:1, now that we have a better understanding of God's mercy?
4. The second step in worshipful prayer is thanking and praising Jesus for His salvation. In your own words (if you can write them down), describe what His redemption in your life means.

5. Look at Psalm 51:12 in terms of always remembering what Jesus has done for us on the cross. What does the "joy of your salvation" mean?
6. We often gloss over how magnificent the majesty of God really is. Why do you think it is important in prayer?
7. "Adoration does not exhaust itself in pleasing our emotions," is a very strong comment. What does it mean?

5
THE ENGAGEMENT—CONFESSION

"The garden of spices is sprinkled with red flowers."
–Heinrich Seuse.

"It is a great and rare thing to have forgiveness in God discovered in a sinful soul. It is a pure Gospel truth, that has no shadow, footstep, nor intimation elsewhere. The whole creation has not the least obscure impression left on it."
–John Owen.

"Before His breath, the bands that held me fall and shrivel up in flame. He bears my name on His wounded hands, on His heart my name. I wait, my soul does wait for Him who on His shoulder hears the key; I sit fast bound, and yet not desolate; my mighty Lord is free. Be lifted up, door of everlasting strength! the Lord on high Has gone, and captive led for evermore My long captivity."
–Dora Greenwell.

"*If we confess our sins, he is faithful and just to forgive us our sins and to cleanse us from all unrighteousness*" (1 John 1:9). Confession of sin is the first act of an awakened sinner, the first sign of a soft spirit. When God looks for a place to live in, He prepares "*a broken and a contrite heart*" (Psalm 51:17). The altar of reconciliation stands at the entrance of the New Testament temple. From the altar, the worshiper carries on through, past the washing basin, to the appointed place of meeting the blood-stained mercy seat.

But now we are speaking about the confession of sin for us who are already justified, having been accepted in Jesus. Though we are children, we are still sinners. And if we walk in the light, we are still conscious—as we never were before being born again—of our wicked guilt and evil sin. For now, we bring our transgressions and wrongs into the light of God's face, and holding them up before Him, we cry, "*Against you, you only, have I sinned and done what is evil in your sight, so that you may be justified in your words and blameless in your judgment*" (Psalm 51:4).

Confession of sin should be explicit and clear. "The care of Christianity is for particulars," says Bishop Warburton. The ritual law in Israel which provided for the transferring of sins on the Day of Atonement assumed that confession would be accurate: "*And Aaron shall lay both his hands on the head of the live goat, and confess over it all the iniquities of the people of Israel, and all their transgressions, all their sins*" (Lev. 16:21).

In private sacrifices, while the hands of the person performing the offering (Lev. 1:4) were laid on the victim, the following prayer was recited: "I call on You, O Jehovah: I have sinned, I have done perversely, I have rebelled, I have committed;" then the sins were named, and the worshiper continued, "but I return in repentance: let this be for my atonement." Standing beside the ruins of Jericho, Joshua said to Achan, "*My son, give glory to the Lord God of Israel and give praise to him. And tell me now what you have done; do not hide it from me." And Achan answered Joshua, "Truly I have sinned against the Lord God of Israel, and this is what I did...*" (Josh. 7:19-20).

The promise of the New Testament is just as accurate and clear: "*If we confess our sins, he is faithful and just to forgive us our sins and to cleanse us from all unrighteousness*" (I John 1:9). A wise old writer said, "A child of God will confess sin specifically; a weak Christian will confess sin by wholesale; he will acknowledge he is a sinner in general; whereas David pointed with his finger to the sore: '*I sinned, and done **this** evil in Your sight*' (Psalm 51:4 NKJV)[31]; he doesn't say, 'I have done evil,' but '***this** evil*.' He points to his offense."

In our daily commitments and tasks, when our conscience tells us that we have sinned, we should confess our guilt at once, claim the cleansing of the blood of Jesus by faith, and wash our hands in innocence. After, as soon as we have an opportunity, we should examine the wrong that we have done. As we look at it with God, we will be shocked at how sinful it is, more than when we were carrying out the deed. And if the sin is one which we have committed before, one that we are often tempted or weak in, we must bring ourselves in faith before the mercy of God, pleading with Him in Jesus' name that we might never grieve Him in that way again.[32]

As our hearts grow softer in the presence of God, remembering our former sins which we have already acknowledged and have been forgiven of, will mark our conscience with a fresh stain every now and then. In such a case, nature seems to teach us that we should beg again for the pardoning grace of God. For we bow, not before the judgment seat of the Divine Lawgiver, but before our Father, to whom we have been reconciled through Jesus. A more adequate understanding of the offense which we have committed should be followed by a deeper repentance for the wrong that we have done. Under the Holy Spirit's guidance we will be led to pray, *"Remember not the sins of my youth"* (Psalm 25:7), even though these have long since been dealt with and done away. The conviction of our sin will naturally prompt us to confess. When such persuasions are ignored, the Spirit who has brought that conviction to us is grieved.

"My sins, my sins, my Savior, How sad on You they fall;

While through Your gentle patience I ten-fold feel them all.

"I know they are forgiven, But still their pain to me

Is all the grief and anguish they laid, my Lord, on Thee."

IT'S EXTREMELY important that in everything we do in the secret chamber, we should surrender ourselves to the influence of the Comforter because it is only by Him that we can pray with acceptance. An important warning about this has been noted by Ralph Erskine.

In his diary, on January 23, 1733, he writes: "This morning I was motivated in prayer, and strengthened to hope in the Lord. At the beginning of my prayer, I had a clear and sure realization of God in Christ as the fountain of my life, the strength of my life, the joy of my life; and that my life did not deserve that name unless He Himself were my life. But here, remembering my own sinfulness, vileness, and corruption, I began to acknowledge my wickedness; and the sweetness I had felt, failed and wore off. I learned this lesson: the sweet influence of the Spirit shouldn't be obstructed through false humility and ungodly sorrow; otherwise, the Lord may be provoked to withdraw."

When Thomas Boston found himself in danger of giving in to pride, he took a look at his black feet.[33] It would be good for us to do the same, but never to lose our assurance of sonship or our sense of the preciousness of Jesus. As Rutherford reminds us, "There is no legalistic music in heaven: there, the only song is, 'Worthy is the Lamb.'" And the blood of ransom has atoned for **all sin.**

Christians from before used to observe with thankfulness the occasions when they were able to show "a penitential mourning for sin." At other times they would regret the deadness in their hearts, but they never used this as an excuse to pray less. On the contrary, they were very clear that with the attitude of a relentless "wrestler at the throne of grace," who was convinced that he would never stop from mentioning "and confessing his sins until his heart was melted in contrition and penitential sorrow."

For such deadness of heart, there may be many explanations.

The person who once was like a flame of fire in his Master's service may have allowed the passion of his first love to fade because it ran out of fuel or was not watched carefully enough until only a little heap of gray ashes are left to smolder on the altar of his love. His greatest sorrow is that he has no sorrow for sin, his heaviest burden is that he is not burdened.

Someone hanging in agony over the edge of a cliff, cried out "Oh, that I was once again under the fear of Christ," for he realized that a cold heart towards Jesus is more dangerous and intolerable than his present predicament. Those who are in such a position are often nearer to the Savior than they know. Shepard of New England, speaking from his own experience, says: "More are drawn to Christ under the sense of a dead, blind heart, than by all sorrows, humiliations, and terrors."

What we feel and think is deadness or lack of life in our heart might be the work of the Holy Spirit, convincing us of sins that we have not yet noticed. As we look at the Milky Way and see the stars only as a blurry mist, we become conscious of the many sins we are hardly aware of, like reflections on the sky. But when we look through a telescope at the nebulous drift, it becomes clearer as a cluster of stars, almost infinite in number. And when we examine in the secret place of prayer, the cloud which darkens the face of God, it scatters and breaks into a multitude of sins.

If, in that time of prayer, we have no living communication with God, let us beg as the Psalms teach us, *"Search me, O*

God, and know my heart! Try me and know my thoughts! And see if there be any grievous way in me, and lead me in the way everlasting" (Psalm 139:23-24). The One who will *"search Jerusalem with lamps"* (Zeph. 1:12) will examine us, will test us as silver is proved, will sift us as wheat. He will bring up from the forgotten depths of our nature all that is against Jesus, and bring every thought to the obedience of His will.

Deadness of heart may also come from thinking about our many sins of neglecting duties, opportunities missed, grace disregarded. Often, when we kneel in prayer, "the lost years cry out." What was said about Archbishop Ussher might be said about many Christians—"He prayed often, and with great humility, that God would forgive him his sins of omission, and his failings in his duty." Each day is a ship to be loaded with holy activities and sincere efforts before it pulls up the anchor and sets sail for the eternal shores. How many hours we waste! How many opportunities we lose! How many precious gifts of God we squander! The world passes away and its fashion fades.

But something lies even deeper in the heart than even secret sin—natural sinfulness, the body of death. When we acknowledge the evil of our nature, we should try and speak according to our experience. The facts can't be exaggerated, but we can easily overstate them. As we grow in grace, as we become used to holding even the smallest thought or feeling before God's piercing pure light, as we open the hidden corners of our lives to the influence of the Holy Spirit, we are led into a greater understanding of wickedness of our inherent sin, until we cry out with Ezra, *"O my God, I am ashamed and blush to lift my face to you, my God"* (Ezra 9:6).

When Martin Luther's inborn sinfulness revealed itself in dreadful ways, so forcefully and terrifying that "the very venom of them drank up his spirits, and his body seemed dead, that neither speech, sense, blood, or heat appeared in him." On a day of special fasting and prayer Thomas Shepard, of Cambridge, Connecticut, wrote: "November 3rd. I saw sin as my greatest evil; and that I was vile; but only God was good, whom my sins did cancel. And I saw what cause I had to hate myself...The Lord also gave me some glimpse of myself; a good day and time it was for me...I went to God and rested on Him...I began to consider whether all the country was not worse off for my sins. And I saw it was. And this was a humbling thought to me."

President Edwards had an amazing discovery of the beauty and glory of Jesus. After recording it in his diary, he continues: "My wickedness, as I am in myself, has long appeared to me perfectly indescribable, swallowing up all thought and imagination, like an infinite river, or mountains over my head. I don't know how better to express my sins, than by heaping infinite upon infinite, and multiplying infinite by infinite. For many years these expressions have been in my mind and my mouth. Infinite upon infinite! Infinite upon infinite!" When Dr. John Duncan was close to death, he remarked with great sincerity, "I am thinking with horror of the carnal mind, enmity against God. I never see it but it produces horror, even bodily sickness."

These are solemn experiences. Perhaps God leads a few of us through waters that are wild and deep. We can't follow unless He points the way. More than that, we must never imitate or manufacture something we have never experienced for ourselves when we are confessing before God. But let us, as far as God has revealed it to us, confess the deep sin of our nature. It has been said[34] that the only "sign of someone being in Jesus that Satan cannot counterfeit" is the grief and sorrow which true Christians go through when God reveals the sinfulness of their natural, inherent sin.

But, the love of Jesus sometimes fills our hearts so much that, though we still remember our sin, the sense of sin is lost—swallowed up in a vast ocean of peace and grace. Such incredible moments of the living God visiting us, are just a prelude to the joy of heaven. For the song of the redeemed in glory is not like the praises sung on earth, because even though it also celebrates the death of the Lamb of God, there is no more mention of sin. All the poisonous fruits of our iniquity have been killed. All the bitter consequences of our evil deeds have been canceled. And the only signs of sin that are found in heaven are the scarred feet and hands and side of the Redeemer. So, when those who are saved recall their former transgressions, they look to Christ; and the remembrance of sin dies in the love of Him who wore the crown of thorns and endured the cross.

"The filthier was the error, The sadder was the fall,

The greater are the praises of Him who pardoned all."

Study Guide

According to McIntyre, this is the second step we can follow after having entered in through the door of worship. Confession is never an easy task unless we just treat it as a duty and repeat our sins without any conviction. Having a sincere and open heart, as we have seen in the chapters before, is the key to entering into God's presence. This is especially true when it comes to confessing and admitting our weaknesses and wrongs before Him.

Again, you are encouraged to keep notes—even of your sins! It often helps us to see them in black and white staring back at us. But be careful who you share what with! Some people don't have the grace to deal with sins and sinners in love. Rather, let the Holy Spirit guide you to the right person— elder, pastor, counselor—that can walk a path with you as God begins setting you free, especially from things that have held you captive for so long.

1. Why do you think confessing our sins is required when, according to Psalm 139, God already knows our thoughts and words before we say them?
2. Read Psalm 51, King David's record of coming before God and confessing. What is meant by a "broken and contrite" heart? Why is this necessary?
3. Why do you think McIntyre spends so long discussing the need to confess sins explicitly or specifically, rather than generally?
4. What is the difference between "secret sins" and "natural sinfulness?"
5. What do you understand by this term "deadness of heart?" Look at Psalm 95:8 and Hebrews 3:15.

6. Is it not a contradiction to always acknowledging our sin, or having it before us, when we are called to live in freedom?
7. Read James 5:16. What do you understand from this verse in terms of what we have been looking at?

6
THE ENGAGEMENT—REQUEST

"Make me sensible of real answers to actual requests, as evidence of an interchange between myself on earth and my Savior in heaven."
–Thomas Chalmers.

"O brother, pray; in spite of Satan, pray; spend hours in prayer; rather neglect friends than not pray; rather fast, and lose breakfast, dinner, tea, and supper—and sleep —than not pray. And we must not talk about prayer, we must pray with purpose and sincerity. The Lord is near. He comes quietly while the bridesmaids sleep."
–A. A. Bonar.

"The main lesson about prayer is just this: Do it! Do it! Do it! You want to be taught to pray. My answer is: Pray and never faint, and then you shall never fail. There is no possibility. You cannot fail; a sense of real want is the very root of prayer."
–John Laidlaw.

Once, when Dr. Moody Stuart was in Huntly, Duncan Matheson took him to see some sincere and committed Christians. He visited, among others, an aged woman who was a very different 'character.' Before leaving, he prayed with her; and she emphasized each request with a loud comment or acceptance. At the end of his prayer, he asked that God, according to His promise, would give her "all things." The old lady interrupted by saying, "All things, no, that would be a lift." The mix of comfort and doubt that was revealed by her words is characteristic of the faith of many other Christians when they are brought face to face with some great promise connected to believing prayer:

- "And whatever you ask in prayer, you will receive, if you have faith" (Matt. 21:22)
- "Therefore I tell you, whatever you ask in prayer, believe that you have received it, and it will be yours" (Mark 11:24)
- "If you abide in me, and my words abide in you, ask whatever you wish, and it will be done for you" (John 15:7).

It's reasonable to think that He who did not spare His own Son will also freely give us all things. But it's so hard to believe that He will. As Dr. Moody Stuart says, the controversy is between the mustard seed and the mountain: "The trial is whether the mountain shall bury the mustard seed, or if the mustard seed will cast the mountain into the sea." The mustard seed is so small, and the mountain so great, that faith is sometimes hard to find. It's literally the gift of God, His persuasion, the fruit of much spiritual instruction and discipline. It's seeing things in a clearer light than in an earthly light.

The prayer of faith, like a plant that is rooted in fruitful soil, draws its goodness from a character that has been brought into conformity with the mind of Christ.

1. It's submitted to His will—*"And this is the confidence that we have toward him, that if we ask anything according to his will he hears us"* (1 John 5:14).
2. It's in line with the interests of Jesus—*"Whatever you ask in my name, this I will do, that the Father may be glorified in the Son"* (John 14:13).
3. It's instructed in the truth—*"If you abide in me, and my words abide in you, ask whatever you wish, and it will be done for you"* (John 15:7).
4. It's motivated by the Spirit—*"Now to him who is able to do far more abundantly than all that we ask or think, according to the power at work within us"* (Eph. 3:20).
5. It's filled with love and mercy—*"And whenever you stand praying, forgive, if you have anything against anyone, so that your Father also who is in heaven may forgive you your trespasses"* (Mark 11:25).
6. It's accompanied by obedience—*"And whatever we ask we receive from him, because we keep his commandments and do what pleases him"* (1 John 3:22).
7. It's so sincere that it won't accept denial—*"And I tell you, ask, and it will be given to you; seek, and you will find; knock, and it will be opened to you"* (Luke 11:9).

It goes out to look for, and to speed up its answer, "*the prayer of a righteous person has great power as it is working*" (James 5:16).[35]

But, although the prayer of faith comes from a God-given character, there is nothing mysterious in the act of faith. It's simply an assurance that relies on a sufficient guarantee:

1. In the first place, the guarantee of faith is the Bible. The promises of God are letters of credit, drawn on the bank of heaven, to be honored immediately. Some time ago, a stash of Bank of England notes was stolen, but they were not signed, and therefore of no value. But the promises of God are all backed by His eternal reputation and are countersigned in the blood of the cross. They are not subject to discount; those who present them will receive their full face value. "*For I am the Lord; I will speak the word that I will speak, and it will be performed*" (Ezek. 12:25).
2. The Bible rests on God's character. Therefore we are taught to pray, "*O Lord, for your name's sake*" (Jer 17:7). God is our Father, and He knows the things that we need. He is our God in covenant—our own God—and He will bless us. He is the God and Father of our Lord Jesus Christ, and He will secure for His beloved Son the inheritance that He has been purchased in blood. He is the source of blessing, from whom the Comforter proceeds, and the prayer that He inspires, He will fulfill.

In the prayers of Daniel the prophet, we have an example of requests established on this double guarantee. He *"perceived in the books the number of years that, according to the word of the Lord to Jeremiah the prophet, must pass before the end of the desolations of Jerusalem, namely, seventy years"* (Dan 9:2).

But the prophet doesn't place His trust only on the promise; he presses into everything that is due to God's character: *"Now therefore, O our God, listen to the prayer of your servant and to his pleas for mercy, and for your own sake, O Lord, make your face to shine upon your sanctuary, which is desolate. O my God, incline your ear and hear. Open your eyes and see our desolations, and the city that is called by your name. For we do not present our pleas before you because of our righteousness, but because of your great mercy. O Lord, hear; O Lord, forgive. O Lord, pay attention and act. Delay not, for your own sake, O my God, because your city and your people are called by your name"* (Dan. 9:17-19).

But someone might object and argue that if our Father knows what we need before we even ask Him for it, and if it's His good pleasure to give us the kingdom, is it still necessary to request these things specifically from Him? The simplest answer to that question is that we are instructed to do so. In the Old Testament we read, *"Thus says the Lord God: This also I will let the house of Israel ask me to do for them"* (Ez. 36:37). And in the New Testament, *"In everything by prayer and supplication with thanksgiving let your requests be made known to God"* (Phil 4:9).

We have a striking explanation of how this Divine law works in the case of Elijah:

- He had been incredibly loyal to God and had fulfilled all the conditions needed to secure and maintain fellowship with the Holy One—"*The Lord of hosts lives, before whom I stand*" (1 Kings 18:15).
- He had won Israel back to the covenant allegiance —"*And when all the people saw it, they fell on their faces and said, 'The Lord, he is God; the Lord, he is God'*" (1 Kings 18:39).
- He had received and acted on a definite promise —"*Go, show yourself to Ahab, and I will send rain upon the earth*" (1 Kings 18:151).
- He had the assurance that God's answer to his prolonged prayer demand was already on its way, "*...there is a sound of the rushing of rain*" (1 Kings 18:41).

Even so, he did not stop praying—he could not until the skies grew dark with the gathering storm.

It's possible, however, to suggest certain reasons why we should persevere to specifically request those blessings which are already ours in Christ.

1. By prayer, our continued and humble dependence on the grace of God is secured. If the gifts of the covenant came to us without having to ask for them, we might be tempted to think we are independent of God, and say, "*My power and the might of my hand have gotten me this wealth*"[36] (Deut. 8:17).
2. The Lord desires for us to communicate with Him.[37] The reluctance of our natural, carnal hearts to stay in God's presence is terrible. We would rather speak of

Him than to Him. How often has to remind and rebuke us, by saying, as the "*companions listening for your voice; let me hear it*" (Song 8:13). A father will cherish a badly spelled, paint-splotched letter from his little child because it is a pledge and seal of love.[38] How precious in God's eyes are the prayers of His children.

3. There is so much that needs to be accomplished in us before we are worthy to receive the gifts we want. God works this preparation of our hearts often by delaying giving us what we ask for at that moment. In this way, He keeps us in the truth of His presence until we are brought into a spiritual understanding of the will of Christ for us in this respect. If a friend, out of his way (Luke 11:6), comes to us, hungry, and asks for the bread of life, and we have nothing to give, we must go to God who has the full storeroom of blessings. And if it seems that He is denying our request or not answering, it's only that we may understand the nature of the blessing we seek, and be made ready to receive it at the right time and in the right attitude.

4. Again, we are called to be co-workers with God, in prayer, as in all other ministries. The exalted Savior lives to make intercession; and to us, He says, "*Remain here, and watch with me*" (Matt. 26:38). There is a great work to be done in the hearts of men, there is a fierce battle to be fought against spiritual wickedness in heavenly places. Demons are to be cast out, the power of hell to be restrained, and the works of the devil to be destroyed. It's only by prayer that

we shall be able to cooperate with the Captain of the Lord's host and accomplish these.[39]

"God spoke, and gave us the word to keep;

Told us never fold the hands, nor sleep

In a faithless world—to watch and ward,

Till Christ at the end relieves our guard.

By His servant Moses the watch was set;

Though we are near the cock-crow, we keep it yet."

WHEN PRAYER RISES to its true level, self, with all its concerns and needs, is momentarily forgotten, and the interests of Jesus fill and sometimes overwhelm the heart. Then prayer becomes urgent and intense. Luther was said to have prayed "with as much reverence as if he were praying to God, and with as much boldness as if he had been speaking to a friend."

One person remarked that in Guthrie of Fenwick's prayers "every word would fill a corn measure." Livingstone said that when Robert Bruce prayed, "every sentence was like a strong bolt shot up to heaven." The biography of Richard Baxter tells us that in prayer, his spirit "took wing for heaven." Similar terms were used to describe Archbishop Leighton, how "his manner of praying was so earnest and importunate as proved that his soul mounted up to God in the flame of his own aspirations."

Henry Martyn wrote in his diary that, having set apart a day for fasting, he began to pray for God's kingdom to come on earth, mentioning India specifically. He received such a great investment and had such energy and delight in prayer that he had never experienced before. He added that his "whole soul wrestled with God. I did not know how to stop crying for Him to fulfill His promises, mainly pleading His own glorious power."

How much of the revival of Central Africa is not owed to the prayers of David Livingstone? He never saw the healing of "the open sore;" he had no idea how much Christianity would spread in "the dark continent." But the record of his prayers is clear and evident. His journals show us a little glimpse of his lonely quiet times, his daily and nightly intercessions. He lived praying for Africa, and when he felt death taking hold of his body, he crept out of bed, and as he knelt on the floor of the simple grass hut in Chitambo's village in Ilala, his heart went up to God in prayer.

He died, his biography says, "in the act of praying in that reverential attitude that he was always so particular about; commending his own spirit, and all his dear ones, as was his custom, into the hands of his Savior, and commending Africa —his own dear Africa—with all her woes, and sins, and wrongs, to the Avenger of the oppressed, and the Redeemer of the lost."

Study Guide

Often we start with requests in prayer. But here we find that one of the best ways to enter into prayer is to see God first and acknowledge Him, then confess our shortcomings and weaknesses, and finally to bring our petitions to the Lord.

As you will have noticed, David McIntyre sprinkles his writings with many verses, making it a very biblical-based approach. Often, he just quotes a short excerpt to emphasize the point being made. It is very useful to read this book with your Bible close by, and instead of just absorbing the author's words, find the verse references and read them in context. This will give a greater understanding of what is said.

If your Bible has a concordance or a reference list, you may find extra verses or clarification that will certainly deepen your study of the topic. You don't have to stick to the questions listed here if you feel that your own investigation is leading you into a more profound revelation—in fact, this is encouraged.

1. Why do you think 'Requests' are listed third in the prayer engagement list?
2. McIntyre talks about a "mix of comfort and doubt" when we ask God for things. Do you find this in your own prayer life? Why?
3. Matt. 21:22, Mark 11:24, John 14:13, John 15:7, 1 John 3:22 all use the word 'whatever.' When you read these, what do you understand, and what does it make you feel about asking for things?
4. Faith is an assurance that relies on a two-part guarantee, according to this chapter. What are these elements?

5. Again, we find the argument that if God knows what we will ask, and wants to reward us, why bother praying? What is the simple answer McIntyre gives?
6. There is a call to keep on praying and not give up when we don't initially receive an answer. What are the four reasons stated by the author?
7. Have you ever prayed for something specific for a long period of time? Did you give up or carry on? What was the outcome?

7

THE HIDDEN RICHES OF THE SECRET PLACE

"Prayer is the means by which we obtain all the graces which rain down on us from the Divine Fountain of Goodness and Love."
–Laurence Scupoli.

"There was a poor widow in that countryside, as I came through, that was worth many of you. She was asked, 'How did you do in this evil time?' 'I do very well,' she said, 'I get more from one verse of the Bible now than I did before. He has given me the keys of the pantry-door, and told me to take my fill."
–Alexander Peden.

"The consolation of Scriptures consists of this, that reading in them the promises of God, we do confirm, and fortify ourselves in Hope. There promising to us that which is given to one to whom a Lord promises by his Letters an income, who maintains himself in the Hope to have that revenue through patience, fortifying his heart more and more through hope, when it seems to him that the accomplishment of

the promise is delayed, not departing from his hope, and comforting himself with the Letter of the Lord."
–Juan de Valds (Nicholas Ferrar's Translation).

The verse, Matthew 6:4, that we have been reading, says that God *"will reward you,"* or in some older translations, instead of reward, uses the word 'recompense.' The reward of praying is, firstly, personal and private; it is *"treasures...in secret places"* (Isa. 45:3). Then, as it passes into life and is acted on, it is shown to everyone. The Father who is in secret, and who sees in secret, openly rewards His servants.

In John Bunyan's *Pilgrim's Progress*, we read that when the pilgrims had almost reached the end of the enchanted ground, "they perceived that before them was a solemn noise, as of one that was much concerned. So they went on, and looked before them; and, behold, they saw, as they thought, a man on his knees, with his hands and eyes lifted up, and speaking, as they thought, earnestly to one that was above. They drew near, but could not tell what he said; so they were quiet until he had finished. When he had finished, he got up, and began to run towards the Celestial City."

This is the first reward of the secret place; through prayer, our good character is awakened, and holiness is worked in us. "Holiness," says Hewitson, "is a habit of mind—a continual placing of the Lord before one's eyes, a constant walking with God as one with whom we are agreed." And in achieving and maintaining continuous communion, "Prayer is amongst duties, as faith is amongst graces." Richard Sibbes reminds us that "Prayer exercises all the characteristics of the Spirit," and Flavel confirms the sentence: "You must strive," he writes, "to excel in this, for no grace in or out of service can thrive without it." Berridge affirms that "all decay begins in the closet; no heart thrives without much secret converse with God, and nothing will make amends for lacking it." On the other hand, he acknowledges, "I never rose from secret prayer without some stirring. Even when I started off with heaviness or reluctance, the Lord is pleased in mercy to meet me in it." Similarly, Fraser of Brea declares, "I find myself better and worse as I decay and increase in prayer."

If prayer is restricted, even if it is restricted by our devotion to other tasks in the ministry, the health of our hearts is reduced. In his diary, Henry Martyn regrets that the "lack of private devotional reading and shortness of prayer, through incessant sermon-making, had produced much strangeness" between God and his heart. Communion with God is the requirement for spiritual growth. It is the soil in which all the virtues of the Christian life root themselves. If the virtues were the work of man, we might perfect them one by one, but they are the fruit of the Spirit, and grow together in one common life. When Philip Saphir became a Christian, he said, "I have found a religion for my whole nature." Holiness is the harmonious perfection, the wholeness of the soul.

As we abide in Christ, we shouldn't allow ourselves to be discouraged by how slowly it seems we are advancing in grace. In nature, growth carries on at different speeds. Sibbes compares the progressive sanctification of Christians to the growth of herbs and trees that "grow at the root in winter, in the leaf in summer, and the seed in autumn." The first of these forms of development seems very slow; the second is more rapid; the third rushes on to full maturity. In a few days of early autumn, a field of grain will seem to ripen more than in weeks of midsummer.

Communion with God reveals the excellence of His character to us, and by seeing Him our hearts are transformed. Holiness is conformity to Christ, and this is only possible by a growing intimacy with Him. It's obvious that this one aspect can open up many different avenues and topics to look at, but for now, we will only indicate one or two of the many directions in which it applies.

1. Firstly, the habit of praying produces a remarkable peace in our spirit. To use Bengel's phrase, we are "built up into a recollected consciousness of God."

When we look into the quiet eyes of Him sitting on the throne, the shaking of our spirit stops and is peaceful. Pharaoh, the king of Egypt, is just a loud noise; and the valley of the shadow of death is filled with songs of praise. Storms may rage beneath us, but the sky above is blue. We take our place with Christ in heavenly places; we dwell in the rest of God. "Here I lie," said Thomas Halyburton when he was very close to death, "pained without pain, without strength yet strong." Seguier, a French Protestant, who was sentenced to death, was mockingly asked by one of his guards how he felt. He replied, "My soul is like a garden, full of shelter and fountains."

There are towns in Europe that would be almost unbearably hot in midsummer if it weren't for the rivers flowing down from the ice fields of Switzerland, bringing a cool and refreshing air during the sweltering noon. In the same way, the river of the water of life, that flows from under the throne of God and the Lamb, makes the city of God glad. Jeremy Taylor put it so well by saying, "Prayer is the peace of our spirits, the stillness of our thoughts, the evenness of our recollection, the seat of our meditation, the rest of our cares, and the calm of our tempest."[40]

1. Again, those who continually pray are taught to rule their lives according to the will of God. This effect follows naturally from the former point, for "all noble, moral energy roots itself in moral calm."

Prayer is the declaration of our dependence as creatures on a Creator. For us as Christians, we have to acknowledge that we are not our own, but because of the great atonement, we are the "purchased possession" of the Son of God.

Pius IV, hearing of John Calvin's death, exclaimed: "Ah, the strength of that proud heretic lay in this, that riches and honor were nothing to him." David Livingstone, in the heart of darkest Africa, wrote in his Journal, "My Jesus, my King, my Life, my All, I again dedicate my whole self to You." Bengel spoke in the name of all Christians when he said, "All I am and have, both in principle and practice, is to be summed up in this one expression—'The Lord's property.' My belonging totally to Christ as my Savior is all my salvation and all my desire. I have no other glory than this, and I want no other." Afterward, when he was close to dying, the following words were spoken over him, "Lord Jesus, to You I live, to You I suffer, to You I die. Yours I am in death and in life; save and bless me, O Savior, forever and ever. Amen."

When the words, "Yours I am" were said, he put his right hand on his heart, as a sign of his full and unreserved agreement. And then he fell asleep in Jesus.

This is the normal attitude of a redeemed soul, an attitude that prayer acknowledges and confirms.

More than that, in prayer we present ourselves to God, holding our own motives before Him in His clear light, and weighing them up according to His will. So, our thoughts and feelings are classified into different groups (as in the old process of polishing or smoothing). Those that rise up towards the honor of God are given priority over those that sink down towards the gratification of self. This is how all the major decisions of our lives should be prepared.

In prayer, Jacob became Israel; in prayer, Daniel saw the day of Jesus, and was glad; in prayer, Saul of Tarsus received his commission to go out to all the Gentiles; in prayer, the Son of Man accomplished His obedience, and embraced His cross. However, it doesn't always happen that the main points of life are recognized as you are praying. Helmholtz, the celebrated physicist, used to say that his greatest discoveries didn't come to him in the laboratory, but when he was walking, perhaps along a country road, when his mind was open and free. His discoveries only registered themselves in his brain then; they were really brought to birth in the laboratory. And whether it's in the place of prayer, or somewhere else, that life's great decisions are made, without a doubt, it's in the secret place and silent hour of prayer that characters are molded and careers determined.

In his Autobiography, George Muller gives an incredible testimony: "I cannot remember, in all my Christian life, a period now (in March, 1895) of sixty-nine years and four months, that I ever **sincerely** and **patiently** sought to know the will of God by the teaching of the Holy Spirit, through the instrumentality of the Word of God, but I have **always** been directed accurately. But if honesty of heart and uprightness before God were lacking, or if I did not patiently wait before God for instruction, or if I preferred the counsel of my fellow-men to the declarations of the Word of the Living God, I made great mistakes."

As we present ourselves before the Lord in prayer, we open our hearts to the Holy Spirit when we yield to the inner impulse, and God's energy commands our being. Our plans, if we have made them according to our human wisdom, are put to one side, and the purpose of God in relation to our lives is accepted. As we are Spirit-born, let us be Spirit-controlled: *"If we live by the Spirit, let us also keep in step with the Spirit"* (Gal 5:25).

1. Through our acceptance of the will of God for our lives, we are led into a richer influence and wider usefulness.

Montalembert once complained to Lacordaire, "How little it is that man can do for his fellows! Of all his miseries this is the greatest." It is true that we can do very little for one another by our ordinary human means, but a lot can be done by prayer. Tennyson's words in this aspect are so true: "More things are wrought by prayer than this world dreams of."

Prayer brings God's omnipotence into our everyday events of life. We ask, and receive, and our joy is full.

An English scholar once said that those who helped him the most were not learned theologians nor eloquent preachers, but holy men and women who walked with God, and unconsciously revealed the raw, plain goodness that the Holy Spirit had produced in them. Those godly people had fixed their eyes on Jesus until they were changed into His image; they had waited on the Mount of God until His divine glory shone on their faces.

Traditional history tells us that Columbia, the Celtic missionary, Ruysbroek, the recluse of Groenendaal, John Welsh of Ayr, and many others, were covered in a soft and tempered glow as they prayed. Of course, such stories were created by remembering those lives that had been transformed and changed.

"I saw a Saint.—How can you tell that

the one you saw was a Saint?—

I saw one like Christ so luminously

by patient deeds of love, his human taint

made his groundwork for humility."

BUT A CHANGED LIFE is not the only gift that God gives to us when we stand in His presence. When Moses came down from Mount Sinai, he was transformed in the eyes of the children of Israel; but he also held in his hands the tablets of the ten commandments—the promises of that covenant, ordered and true, which had been given to him for them. His prayer had saved the chosen people, and the ten commandments were the sign.

John Nelson, hearing someone comparing how much worse John Wesley was to a celebrity preacher of the time, replied, "But he has not waited in the Upper Room as John Wesley has done." It is this waiting in the Upper Room that assures the gift of power. This line of thought leads us on to the theme of our final chapter—The Open Reward.

Study Guide

In the closing chapters of the book, after discussing the need for prayer and the way to pray, and the patterns we can follow, McIntyre outlines the benefits and treasures we find in this spiritual act of communing with God. First, he looks at those rewards that we are often not even actively asking for or pursuing, but are fruits and by-products of us engaging in prayer.

Hopefully, you have benefitted from the study guide and used it to gain a deeper understanding, or do some self-reflection, or stir up discussion in your group. If you have simply read the book, that, too, will give you much to think and talk about. Whichever route you choose, remember that it is only the Holy Spirit who steers us to real spiritual revelation and clearly seeing our state of heart before God. So, read, letting Him open your eyes, mind, and heart.

1. What is the first reward we obtain when we spend time in prayer with God?
2. Read Matthew 6:6 again. It is very specific about rewarding the prayer that is done in 'secret.' Why is this so significant? Why does he then 'openly' reward it?
3. Looking at this, in the context of prayer, what do you understand by Hebrews 11:6?
4. The first of the three aspects looked at in terms of a heart that is transformed, is peace. Explain how and why you think this comes to a person who diligently prays.
5. The second benefit that is achieved without actively looking for it, is submission to God's will. How does praying bring such a characteristic into our lives?
6. The third point is that we influence those around us, simply by spending time with God. Do you know someone like this? Describe them.
7. McIntyre tells us that a changed life is not the only gift we receive when we pray. What is the other gift?

8

THE OPEN REWARD

*"Jesus, Lord God from all eternity,
Whom love of us brought down to shame,
I plead Thy life with Thee,
I plead Thy death, I plead Thy name.
Jesus, Lord God of every living soul,
Thy love exceeds its uttered fame,
Thy will can make us whole,
I plead Thyself. I plead Thy name."*
–Christina Rossetti.

*"No one can believe how powerful prayer is,
and what it is able to affect,
but those who have learned it by experience.
It is a great matter when in extreme
need to take hold of prayer.
I know, whenever I have prayed earnestly
that I have been amply heard,*

and have obtained more than I prayed for.
God indeed sometimes delayed,
but at last, He came."
–Luther.

"*I sought Him in my hour of need;*
(Lord God now hear my prayer!)
For death, He gave me life indeed,
And comfort for despair.
For this, my thanks shall endless be,
Oh thank Him, thank Him now with me,
Give to our God the glory!"
–J. J. Schutz.

In their efforts to explain the personal benefits that are gained from spending time communicating with God, the early Greek Fathers of the Church used the picture of a boat tied to a ship. They said that if a person had to pull on the rope, the ship would not move at all, but the boat would immediately respond to the movement. Apparently, they forgot, or maybe didn't know, that in physical mechanics, "action and reaction are equal and opposite." The result of the pull would affect the larger vessel as much as the smaller one, although the heavier bulk of the ship would make the displacement much less obvious than it would be on the boat. It's the same in prayer, the influence is reciprocal. As we have seen, there is an increased presence in our lives of all the Christian virtues; but there are also direct answers to requests offered in faith.

If we do not expect to receive answers to our requests, our whole concept of prayer is wrong. "No one asks in earnest," says Trail, "but they will try to prosper. There is no surer and clearer sign of petty prayer than when men are careless about what they get by prayer." And to the same effect, Richard Sibbes writes: "We should watch daily, continue every moment in prayer; strengthen our supplications with arguments from God's Word and promises, and see how our prayers succeed. When we shoot an arrow we look to where it falls; when we send a ship to sea we look for its return; and when we sow we look for a harvest. It is atheistic to pray and not to wait in hope. A sincere Christian will pray, wait, strengthen his heart with the promises, and never leave praying and looking up until God gives him a gracious answer."

And if the answer is delayed, we should ask if the thing that we desire is really according to the will of God; and if we are satisfied that it is, we should continue praying every moment. Bengel judges that "a Christian should not stop praying until his heavenly Father allows him to stop, by permitting him to obtain something." And George Muller drew encouragement from the fact that he was able to persevere in prayer daily, for twenty-nine years, for a certain spiritual blessing that was held back from him: "At home and abroad, in this country and foreign lands, in health and sickness, however much occupied, I have been enabled, day by day, by God's help, to bring this matter before Him, and still I do not have the full answer yet. Nevertheless, I look for it. I expect it confidently. The very fact that day after day, and year after year, for twenty-nine years, the Lord has enabled me to continue patiently, believingly, to wait on Him for the blessing, still encourages me further to wait on it; and so I am fully assured that God hears me about this matter, that I have often been enabled to praise Him beforehand for the full answer which I shall ultimately receive for my prayers on this subject."[41]

We should not doubt that any prayers which are in accordance with the will of God shall be answered in full because our confidence is in the Word and Name of Jesus. But there are many requests that we might not be so sure and confident of—they don't stand so clearly in God's will that we are certain about them. And for many of those prayers, they seem to return empty.

- Moses wanted to pass over the Jordan River with the tribes of Israel; but God said to him, *"Enough from you; do not speak to me of this matter again"* (Deut 3:26).
- Paul asked the Lord three times that the thorn in his side might be taken away, but the only response he received was, *"My grace is sufficient for you, for my power is made perfect in weakness"* (2 Cor 12:9).
- John, the disciple whom Jesus loved, encourages us to pray for the salvation of our friends and family, but even as we address ourselves to this holy duty he reminds us that *"there is sin that leads to death"* (1 John 5:16). Apparently, in such circumstances, not even prayer will succeed.

We can be sure that "Whatever is good for God's children they shall have it; for everything is theirs to help them towards heaven; therefore if poverty is good they shall have it; if disgrace or crosses are good they shall have them; for everything is ours to promote our greatest prosperity."[42]

When we pray for temporary blessings, we are sometimes conscious of the special help of the Spirit in our intercession. This is a sign that we can believe our prayer is pleasing to God. But we must be careful not to confuse the desires of our flesh with the promptings of the Spirit. Only those whose eye is focused, and whose whole body is full of light, as a result, can properly distinguish between the impulses of the flesh and of the Spirit.[43]

Paying attention to this warning, we can find encouragement from the sincerity and passion of our requests. John Livingstone made this private note to himself: "After prayer, I look back and summarize what petitions God has put in my mouth, and these I count as blessings promised, and look for their fulfillment." Augustus Toplady says the same thing, but much more boldly: "I can, to the best of my remembrance and belief, truly say that I have never yet had one promise, nor assurance, concerning temporary things, impressed upon me beforehand in a way of communion with God, which the event did not realize. I never, that I know of, knew it to fail in any one single instance."[44]

So, what sort of things should our requests contain? Maximus of Tyre declared that he would not ask the gods for anything but goodness, peace, and hope in death. But as Christians, we may ask our Father for everything that we need, as long as our desires are restrained, and our prayers unselfish. The personal requests that we find in the Lord's

Prayer are very modest and simple—daily bread, forgiveness, and deliverance from the power of sin. Yet these few components make up all the things that pertain to life and godliness.

Bread and water, and a place of shelter are assured to us. Fortress, and fortress provisions![45] But we aren't always reduced to such simplicity of supply: God is so much better than His word. He feeds us with suitable and appropriate food; and if He should ever bring us to a place of hunger, it is only so that our spiritual characters may be made richer.

But man does not live by bread alone. Health and comfort, the joys of home, and the pleasures of knowledge are blessings which we can ask for, and they will not be kept back from us unless our Father judges it best that we should be deprived of them. But if He should not answer our repeated request, and refuse to receive our prayer, we must then reply the same way that Jesus did: "*Abba, Father, all things are possible for you...Yet not what I will, but what you will*" (Mark 14:36).[46] When we reach the end of our journey, if not before, we shall be able to say, "*Not one word has failed of all his good promise*" (1 Kings 8:56).

When we pray for spiritual blessings, we never ask in vain. James Gilmour writes to someone who asked him to explain further, "All I know about the process is just going to God and telling what I want, and asking to be allowed to have it. '*Ask, and it will be given to you; seek, and you will find*' (Matt 7:7). I know no secret but this."

Gilmour carries on, saying, "You say you want to be revived—go directly to Jesus and ask it straight out, and you'll get it straight away. This revived state is not a thing you need to work yourself up into, or need others to help you to rise into, or need to come to England to be operated on, Jesus can make it happen anywhere and does perform it everywhere, whenever a man or woman, or men and women, ask it. "*Ask, and it will be given to you.*" My dear brother, I have learned that the source of many blessings is just to go to Jesus, and tell Him what you need."

A Scottish Covenanter reported that he received more grace in one afternoon, spent in prayer, than during the whole year before. After two days' prayer in the woods of Anwoth, Samuel Rutherford received the spiritual call to be a minister of Jesus Christ. And how many other people who have knelt in an upper room, have received the heavenly baptism of the Holy Spirit. All the storehouses of God open at the voice of faith.

Answers to prayer may always mark the person praying, but they might not be able to convince others that the events which happen are because of the direct intervention of God. Let's take a look at two examples:

"A Christian man once jumped after his boy, who had fallen into the swollen flood of the Wupper River. As he jumped in, he cried, 'Lord, teach me to swim!' He swam skillfully, though he had never tried it before, and saved his child."[47]

Once, when a sudden and terrific hailstorm was pouring down on the fields, and possibly bringing serious damage, a person rushed into Bengel's room, and exclaimed: 'Sir, everything will be destroyed; we shall lose all!' Bengel went calmly to the window, opened it, lifted up his hands to heaven, and said, 'Father, restrain it'; and the storm actually abated from that moment."⁴⁸

Often, however, the reward of prayer is so conspicuous that it is not really possible to ignore the connection between the request and the answer. Let's take a look at this case of charitable institutions founded by their promoters on the promises of God as an example.

The Pietas Hallensis is nothing more than the record of statements granted to Dr. Francke in connection with the orphan houses at Halle. Here is one: "Another time I stood in need of a great sum of money, where even a hundred crowns would not have covered the amount, and yet I saw no way how I might be given the groats we needed. The servant came and showed me the state of lack we were in. I asked him to come again after dinner, and I resolved to lift up my prayers to the Lord for His assistance. When the servant came in again after dinner, I was still in the same place of need, and so appointed him to come in the evening.

In the meantime, a friend of mine had come to see me, and I joined with him in prayers and was moved to praise and magnify the Lord for all His admirable dealings towards mankind, even from the beginning of the world, and the most remarkable events came quickly and clearly to my remembrance while I was praying. I was so elevated in praising and magnifying God, that I insisted on focusing only on that as my present devotion, with no inclination to put forward the many anxious requests that I needed help with at the present moment. After a while, my friend had to leave, and I accompanied him to the door, where I found the servant waiting on one side for the money he wanted, and on the other side a person who brought a hundred and fifty crowns for the support of the hospital."

The history of George Muller's Homes at Ashley Down is written as a vivid reminder for all Christians to read. Mr. Muller, through many trials of faith, encountered one which was especially difficult. Looking back on it many years later, he remembers the Lord's deliverance and adds: "The only inconvenience that we had, in this case, was that our dinner was about half an hour later than usual. Such a thing, as far as I remember, scarcely ever occurred before, and has never occurred since."

William Quarrier balanced the accounts of the Homes at Bridge of Weir every month. If at any time it appeared possible that the balance would be short, he called his co-workers to pray, and most often, the needed funds came in. Just before he died, he testified that he had never been in debt for one hour.

"The God that answers orphanages," exclaimed C. H. Spurgeon, "let Him be God."

Less tangible, but no less obvious, are the answers granted to prayers for the extension of Jesus' kingdom on earth. To illustrate this point properly, you would just have to take a look at the history of the church. It would be wonderful if this was only the beginning of this book and not the end; there are so many examples that could be shared to encourage us!

By prayer, a handful of uneducated and ignorant men, used to working the oar and the rudder, the plow, and the pruning-shears turned the world upside down and spread the name of Jesus beyond the limits of Roman power.

By prayer, the tent-maker of Tarsus won the promiscuous Corinthians over to purity and faith,[49] laid the enduring foundations of Western Christianity, and lifted the name of Jesus high in Nero's very own palace.

The ruined cells on many barren islands in the Scottish seas remind us of the weeks and months of prayer and fasting by which the Celtic missionaries, in the space of one generation, won Caledonia for Christ.

The prayers of Luther and his colleagues sent the great truths of the Gospel flying across Europe as if they were on the wings of angels.

The moorland and the mountains of Scotland are still a witness to the covenant of Christ that heard the prayers of Welsh and Cargill, Guthrie and Blackadder, Peden and Cameron.

Before the great revival in Gallneukirchen broke out, Martin Boos spent hours and days, and often nights, in lonely, agonizing intercession. Afterward, when he preached, his words were like a flame, and the hearts of the people as dry grass that caught alight at his words.

A sermon preached in Clynnog, Caernarvonshire, by Robert Roberts, was the apparent cause of a widespread revival in Wales. It's said that a hundred people were saved as a result. Some days later, a friend of the preacher, John Williams, Dolyddelen, said, "Tell me, Roberts, where did you get that wonderful sermon?" "Come here, John," said Roberts, as he led him to a small room, and continued, "It was here I found that sermon you speak of—on the floor here, all night long, turning backward and forward, with my face sometimes on the earth."

It's always the same. Those who have turned many to righteousness have labored early and late with the weapon called prayer.

Joseph Alleine "was infinitely and insatiably greedy for the conversion of souls." There is a story about him, that says: "At the time of his health, he constantly woke up at or before four 'o'clock...From four until eight he spent time in prayer, holy contemplation, and singing psalms, in which he delighted very much...Sometimes he would put off the routine of conventional duties and devote whole days to these secret exercises, and plan to be alone in some empty house, or else in some quiet, lonely spot in the open valley."

William Grimshaw, the apostle of Yorkshire, was known to have the "custom to rise early in the morning—at five in the winter, and at four in the summer—that he might begin the day with God."

George Whitefield frequently spent whole nights in meditation and prayer, and often rose from his bed in the night to intercede for lost souls. He says: "Whole days and weeks have I spent lying flat on the ground in silent or vocal prayer."

The biographer of Payson observes that "prayer was preeminently the business of his life," and he himself used to strongly assert that he felt sorry for the Christian who could not enter into the meaning of the verse, *"groanings too deep for words"* (Rom. 8 26). It is also said about him, that he "wore the hardwood boards into grooves where his knees pressed so often and so long."

In summary, every gracious work which has been accomplished within the kingdom of God has started, grown, and been completed by prayer.

"What is the secret of this revival?" a person asked Evan Robertsone in 1905. "There is no secret," was the reply, "It is only, 'Ask, and receive.'"

Study Guide

In the last chapter, the benefits of prayer are more obvious than a changed character; they are the very things we seek and ask for, and receive openly and publicly. They could range from a safe trip, good weather, healing from pain to someone being born again. All of them are very specific and the answers to each cannot be mistaken, as we either receive exactly what we ask for or not.

Take your time to work through the questions. Let them simmer in your mind for a while, giving them time to work into your heart as the Holy Spirit brings answers to you that will lead you even deeper.

1. Think of times you received an answer to prayer almost immediately. Now, think of an instance where you only got the reply months or years later. Was

there any difference in the way you prayed or the intensity of your request?
2. Why do you think God sometimes takes His time in answering our prayers?
3. What question does the author say we should ask ourselves when the answer to our prayers is delayed?
4. Why do you think He refuses us, even when we ask in faith and believe? Does this not contradict a verse like Matthew 21:22?
5. McIntyre writes that "when we pray for spiritual blessings we never ask in vain." Why is this different from asking for physical blessings?
6. If you wrote a list of things you wanted from God before reading this book and had to write a new list of requests now, would there be a difference between the two? Why?
7. Name one major revelation of prayer you have received from reading *The Hidden Life of Prayer*.

In having finished reading this book, and working through the study questions, perhaps some of David McIntyre's wisdom has brought more light to you as a Christian in the area of prayer. But, rather than a better understanding and a greater knowledge, the only real way to grow is to allow God Himself to give us a spiritual revelation—a deposit in our hearts that will bear fruit. In the author's words, "Lord, teach us to pray."

FOOTNOTES

1. "Believe me, to pray with all your heart and strength, with reason and the will, to believe vividly that God will listen to your voice through Christ, and, truly, to do the thing that pleases Him; this is the last, the greatest achievement of the Christian's warfare upon the earth. Teach us to pray, O Lord." –Coleridge.
2. Dr. Horton, Verbum Dei, p. 214.
3. "It is a tremendously hard thing to pray right. Yes, it is truly the science of all sciences even to pray so that the heart may approach God with all gracious confidence, and say, 'Our Father, who is in heaven.' For he who can take to himself such confidence of grace is already over the hill of Difficulty and has laid the foundation-stone of the temple of prayer." – Luther, Parting Words (Edin., 1903), p. 73.

"Perfect prayer is not attained by the use of many words, but through deep desire." –Catherine of Siena.

1. "We know the utility of prayer from the efforts of the wicked spirits to distract us during the Divine office, and we experience the fruit of prayer in the defeat of our enemies." –John Climacus, The Holy Ladder of Perfection, xxviii. 64.

"When we go to God by prayer, the devil knows we go to fetch strength against him, and therefore he opposes us all he can." –R. Sibbes, Divine Meditations, 164.

1. "If you find a weariness in this duty, suspect yourself, purge and refine your heart from the love of all sin, and endeavor to put it into a heavenly and spiritual frame; and then you will find this no unpleasant exercise, but full of delight and satisfaction. In the meantime, complain not of the hardness of the duty, but of the untowardness of your own heart." –The Whole Duty of Man (Lond., 1741), p. 122.
2. F. W. H. Myers, Poems.
3. "In our mutual intercourse and conversation—amidst all the busiest scenes of our pilgrimage—we may be moving to and fro on the rapid wing of prayer, of mental prayer—that prayer that lays the whole burden of the heart on a single sigh. A sigh breathed in the Spirit, though inaudible to all around us but God may sanctify every conversation, every event in the history of the day. We must have fellowship at all times either with the spirit of the

world or with the Spirit of God...Prayer will be fatiguing to flesh and blood if uttered aloud and sustained long. Oral prayer, and prayer mentally ordered in words though not uttered aloud, no believer can engage in without ceasing, but there is an undercurrent of prayer that may run continually under the stream of our thoughts, and never weary us. Such prayer is the silent breathing of the Spirit of God, who dwells in our hearts (see Rom. 8:9, and 1 Col. 3:16); it is the temper and habit of the spiritual mind; it is the pulse of our life which is hidden with Christ in God." –Hewitson's Life, pp. 100, 101.

"My mind was greatly fixed on Divine things: almost perpetually in contemplating them. I spent most of my time thinking of Divine things, year after year; often walking alone in the woods, and solitary places, for meditation, soliloquy, and prayer, and converse with God, and it was always my manner to sing my contemplations. I was almost constantly in ejaculatory prayer, wherever I was. Prayer seemed to be natural to me, as the breath by which the inner burnings of my heart were vented." –Jonathan Edwards, Memoirs. chap. i.

"I see that unless I keep up a short prayer every day throughout the whole day, at intervals, I lose the spirit of prayer. I would never lose sight at any hour of the Lamb in the midst of the throne, and if I have this sight, I shall be able to pray. –Andrew A. Bonar, Diary. 7th October 1860.

1. "Is not the name of prayer usually to signify all the service that we ever do to God?" –Hooker, Eccles. Polity, v. 23.
2. Dr. A. B. Davidson, Waiting upon God, p. 14.
3. Compare the sentence of Thomas Hooker, of Hartford—"Prayer is the principal work of a minister, and it is by this he must carry on the rest."
4. "Whoever is diligent in public prayers, and yet negligent in private, it is much to be feared he rather seeks to approve himself to men than to God." –The Whole Duty of Man (Lond., 1741), p. 119.
5. Harvey's The Rise of the Quakers, pp. 73, 74.
6. The Scale of Perfection, I. i. 1.
7. The late Dr. John Paton, of the New Hebrides, tells of such a prayer chamber in his father's modest dwelling—"Our home consisted of a 'but' and a 'ben,' and a middle-room, or chamber, called the 'closet.'...The closet was a very small apartment between the other two, having room only for a bed, a little table, and a chair, with a diminutive window shedding a diminutive light on the scene. This was the sanctuary of that cottage home. There daily, and many times a day, generally after each meal, we saw our father retire, and shut to the door; and we children got to understand, by a sort of spiritual instinct (for the thing was too sacred to be talked about), that prayers were being poured out there for us, as of old by the High Priest within the veil in the Most Holy Place. We occasionally heard the pathetic echoes of a trembling voice, pleading as for life, and we learned to slip in and

out past that door on tip-toe, not to disturb the holy change. The outside world might not know, but we knew where that happy light came from, as of a newborn smile that was always dawning on my father's face: It was a reflection from the Divine Presence, in the consciousness of which he lived. Never, in a temple or cathedral, in a mountain or in the glen, can I hope to feel that the Lord God is more near, more visibly walking and talking with men, than under that humble cottage roof of thatch and oak wattles." –Dr. John G. Paton, Autobiography, pp. 10, 11.

8. "On his return from the West Indies to the Clyde, Hewitson was privileged to lead one of the sailors to Christ. "I am not lacking a closet to pray in," he said one day, as the voyage drew near its termination; "I can just cover my face with my hat, and I am as much alone with God as in a closet." The man had sailed from Antigua, a careless sinner. –Hewitson's Life, p. 283.

9. "Let no man that can find time to spend on his vanities...say he wants time for prayer." –The Whole Duty of Man (Lond. 1741), p. 120.

10. In all his journeyings, John Wesley used to carry with him a little notebook for jottings, the first crude draft of his Journals. On the front page of each successive copy of this memorandum book, he always recorded a resolution to spend two hours daily in private prayer, no evasion or proviso being admitted. Perhaps such a rule may seem to be rigid to some, even to formality. Let no one be bound by another's practice,

but in every case let due provision be made for intercourse with God.
11. "And here I was advised to set up one other sail, for before I prayed only twice a day, I here resolved to set some time apart at mid-day for this effort, and, obeying this, I found the effects to be wonderful." – Memoirs of the Rev. James Fraser (Wodrow), p. 208.
12. But Fraser of Brea gives a caution respecting this which is worth remembering: "Under the pretense of waiting on the Lord for strength, I have been driven to gaze, and neglect the duty itself, when there has been an opportunity; so in preparing for prayer have neglected prayer." –Memoirs, p. 290.
13. "It was a saying of the martyr, Bradford, that be would never leave a duty until he had brought his heart into the frame of the duty; he would not leave confession of sin until his heart was broken for sin; he would not leave petitioning for grace until his heart was quickened and enlivened in a hopeful expectation of more grace; he would not leave the rendering of thanks until his heart was enlarged with the sense of the mercies which lie enjoyed and motivated in the return of praise." –Bickersteth, A Treatise on Prayer, p. 93.
14. "This helping of the Spirit (Rom. 8:26) is very emphatical in the original; as a man taking up a heavy piece of timber by the one end cannot get it up alone until some other man takes it up at the other end, and so helps him; so the poor soul that is pulling and tugging with his own heart, he finds it heavy and dull, like a log in a ditch, and he can do no

good with it, until at last the Spirit of God comes at the other end, and takes the heaviest end of the burden, and so helps the soul to lift it up." –I. Ambrose, Prima Media et Ultima, p. 333.

Père La Combe says: "I have never found anyone who prayed so well as those who had never been taught how. They who have no master in man have one in the Holy Spirit." –Spiritual Maxims, 43.

1. The reader will find a striking passage, hearing on this point, in the Autobiography of George Muller (Lond., 1905), pp. 152, 153.
2. "Always enter into prayer by putting yourself in the Divine Presence" (Francois de Sales). Gaston de Renty defines this position of the soul as "a state of modest presence before God, in which you maintain yourself, looking to His Spirit to suggest what He pleases to you, and receiving it in simplicity and confidence, just as if He were uttering words in your hearing." Avila, a Spanish writer on religion tells us that "we ought to address ourselves to prayer, rather, in order to listen than to speak."
3. "Prayer reveals to us the true state of our soul, for, according to theologians, it is the mirror which shows us our correct portrait." –St. John Climacus, The Holy Ladder of Perfection, xx iii. 38.
4. "The petitions of believers...are echoes, so to speak, of the Master's own words. Their prayer is only some fragment of His teaching transformed into a supplication. It must then be heard, for it is the

expression of His will." –Bishop Westcott, on the verse John 15:7.

5. "Prayer is heard when it passes from the believer's heart to the Redeemer's heart, and is appropriated by the Redeemer, or made His own." –W. H. Hewitson, Life, p. 375.
6. Epictetus, Eph. 1:16.
7. Richard Baxter advises that on Sabbath days we should be briefer in confession and lamentation, and give ourselves more to praise and thanksgiving (Method of Peace and Comfort). It was Grimshaw's custom to begin his morning devotions by singing the doxology. Of Joseph Alleine it was said, "Such was the vehement heavenliness of his spirit, that his favorite employment was praise."
8. Chrysostom, quoted by Thomas Watson.
9. "No doubt the angels think themselves as insufficient for the praises of the Lord as we do." –John Livingstone's Diary, 14 Dec. 1634 (Wodrow Society).
10. Scripture taken from the New King James Version®. Copyright © 1982 by Thomas Nelson. Used by permission. All rights reserved.
11. "Think of the guilt of sin, that you may be humbled. Think of the power of sin, that you may seek strength against it. Think not of the matter of sin...in case you become more and more entangled." –John Owen.
12. The biographer of Charles Simeon, of Cambridge, remarks: "Simeon in his private hours was peculiarly broken and prostrated before the Lord."
13. By Dr. Payson, Lift, p. 79.

14. "In prayer, we tempt God if we ask for that which we do not labor for; our faithful endeavors must second our devotion...If we pray for grace and neglect the spring from whence it comes, how can we succeed? It was a rule in ancient times, 'Lay your hand to the plow, and then pray.' No man should pray without plowing, nor plow without prayer." –R. Sibbes, Divine Meditations, p. 174.
15. "Prayer not only obtains mercies; it sweetens and sanctifies them." –Flavel, Works, v. 351.

"God does not delay to hear our prayers, because He has no mind to give; but that, by enlarging our desires, He may give us a larger abundance." –Anselm of Canterbury.

1. "We must draw from prayer, from resting in it, or trusting on it; a man may preach much, and instead of drawing near to God, or enjoying sweet communion with Christ, he may draw near to prayer, his thoughts may be more on his prayer than on God to whom he prays, and he may live more on his cushion than on Christ; but when a man indeed draws near to God in prayer, he forgets prayer and remembers God, and prayer goes for nothing, but Christ is all." –Isaac Ambrose, Prima Media et Ultima, p. 332.
2. "The brief, childlike letters that were sent to him by them [his sons] were bound up into a paper volume, which he carried about with him during his Mongolian wanderings, and in looking over them he

found an unfailing solace and refreshment." –Life of Gilmour of Mongolia, pp. 241, 251.

3. "It was seven years before William Carey baptized his first convert in India; it was seven years before Judson won his first disciple in Burma; Morrison toiled seven years before the first Chinese man was brought to Christ; Moffat declares that he waited seven years to see the first evident moving of the Holy Spirit on his Bechuanas of Africa; Henry Richards worked seven years on the Congo before the first convert was gained at Banza Manteka." –A. J. Gordon, The Holy Spirit in Missions, pp. 139, 140.

4. Jeremy Taylor, The Return of Prayers. This applies also on a lower level. George Müller writes, "These last three days I have had very little real communion with God, and have therefore been very weak spiritually, and several times have felt irritability of temper. May God in mercy help me to have more secret prayer." –Autobiography, p. 67.

5. On this point, Müller says elsewhere: "It is not enough to begin to pray, nor to pray correctly; nor is it enough to continue for a time to pray; but we must patiently, believingly, continue in prayer until we obtain an answer; and further, we have not only to continue in prayer until the end, but we also have to believe that God does hear us, and will answer our prayers. Most frequently we fail in not continuing in prayer until the blessing is obtained, and in not expecting the blessing." –Autobiography, p. 320.

6. Richard Sibbes Divine Meditations, p. 5.

7. The following extract from the Life of John Howe may serve to point a caution which has sometimes been too lightly heeded: "At that time [in the days of the English Commonwealth] an erroneous opinion, still cherished by a few pious people, respecting the efficacy of a special faith in prayer, pervaded the religious community. The idea was entertained that if a believer was led to seek a favor in prayer, such as the recovery or conversion of a child, or victory on the battlefield, with unusual fervor, and with the strong persuasion that the prayer would be favorably answered, such would certainly be the case. This notion was carried by some to still greater lengths of extravagance until it amounted to a virtual assertion of inspiration. The court of Cromwell was not unfavorable soil for the nourishment of a conceit like this; indeed, it appears to have taken deep hold of the mind of the Protector himself. Thoroughly convinced of its erroneous nature and unhallowed tendencies, and having listened to a sermon at Whitehall, the avowed design of which was to maintain and defend it, Howe felt himself bound in conscience to expose its absurdity when next he should preach before Cromwell. This he did...Cromwell's brow furnished indications of his displeasure during the delivery of the discourse, and a certain coolness in his manner afterward, but the matter was never mentioned between them."
8. This "particular faith in prayer" sometimes engages itself in receiving the answer to prayers offered for spiritual interests. Speaking of the memorable revival

in Kilsyth, of which the first fruits were seen on Tuesday, 23rd July 1839, "a morning fixed from all eternity in Jehovah's counsel as an era in the history of redemption" –William Burns wrote: "I have since heard that some of the people of God in Kilsyth, who had been longing and wrestling for a time of refreshing from the Lord's presence, and who had, during much of the previous night, been travailing in birth for souls, came to the meeting," not only with the hope but with the certain anticipation of God's glorious appearing, from the impressions they had on their own souls of Jehovah's approaching glory and majesty."

9. "Being asked by a lady if he would have bread and a glass of wine, he replied, 'If you please, I'll have bread and a glass of water.' 'Prison fare,' remarked the lady. 'No, fortress provisions: *he will dwell on the heights; his place of defense will be the fortresses of rocks; his bread will be given him; his water will be sure*' (Isa. 33:16). –John Duncan, The Pulpit and Communion Table, p. 37.

10. Mr. D. L. Moody used to say that he thanked God with all his heart that many of his most earnest prayers had not been granted.

11. F. W. Krummacher, Autobiography (Edin., 1869). p. 143.

12. Memoir of J. A. Bengel. by J. C. F. Burk (Lond., 1837), pp. 491, 492.

13. "'The Church of God in Corinth,' a blessed and astounding paradox!"–Bengel.

ABOUT DAVID MCINTYRE

On paper, Dr. Mcintyre's life seems to take a very ordinary route from his years growing up, to being schooled, and then entering into the same profession that his father before him had held. There is not much to be found in his history regarding great travels, huge conferences, or incredible revivals. One may even discount him if you had to compare his achievements to those other great men around him at the time. And yet, his name is still spoken alongside the prominent Christians of his era.

He lived in the presence of God, but rather than being someone who was too spiritual for daily life, he was regarded as a practical man. Rather than getting caught up in the everyday demands, McIntyre used his time in prayer before God to enrich and prepare him for everything. And like Moses, it was evident to many people that he interacted with that he had spent time with his Lord.

David Martin McIntyre was born in Angus, Scotland in 1859. His father, Malcolm, was the minister of the Free Church of Scotland in Monikie, where he married David's mother, the daughter of the previous minister.

David had two siblings, an elder sister named Margaret and an elder brother called Miller Malcolm. However, they both died a few years apart, still fairly young, which left David to grow up as an only child.

His education saw him excel in his studies at New College, the University of Edinburgh, before he set off to London to complete and graduate from the English Presbyterian College. With a doctorate in hand, he went on to gain some training as a missionary under the teaching of Dr. John Kelman McIntyre at St John's Church in Leith. He spent some time in Dundee, Willesden, and Drury Lane, London.

In 1886, he accepted the position as the Presbyterian minister of College Park Church, Kensal Rise, London. He stayed there for five years before returning to Scotland to take over from Andrew Bonar, with whom he had become very close friends. Not only did he assume the role of the minister at Bonar's Finnieston parish in Glasgow, but he also married his daughter, Jane Christian Bonar, two years later.

In 1913, after John Andersen had relinquished his post as head of the college, McIntyre was elected the principal of the Bible Training Institute in Glasgow. At the same time, he was still serving as a minister in his local church, and he made the decision to join the greater body of the Church of Scotland in 1929. In May 1936, after serving Finnieston for 50 years, he and his parish celebrated his jubilee of ministry.

As a prolific writer, he wrote a number of good Christian books, as well as being editor of The King's Writ—A Quarterly Journal of Bible Study during the 1920s. Although, he is most remembered for his work on *The Hidden Life of Prayer*.

David McIntyre passed away on 8 March, 1938, leaving behind the rich legacy of a man who prayed and communed with God.

REFERENCES

Crossway Bibles. (2016). *ESV: Study Bible: English standard version*. Crossway Bibles.

Macintyre, D. (1906). *The hidden life of prayer*.

Nelson, T. (2017). *NKJV Holy Bible*. Thomas Nelson.

www.ingramcontent.com/pod-product-compliance
Lightning Source LLC
LaVergne TN
LVHW020444070526
838199LV00063B/4843